LEARN
Adobe Illustrator CC
for **Graphic Design** and **Illustration**

SECOND EDITION

Adobe Certified Associate Exam Preparation

Chad Chelius
with Rob Schwartz

Adobe

LEARN ADOBE ILLUSTRATOR CC FOR GRAPHIC DESIGN AND ILLUSTRATION, SECOND EDITION
ADOBE CERTIFIED ASSOCIATE EXAM PREPARATION
Chad Chelius
with Rob Schwartz

Adobe Press books is an imprint of Pearson Education, Inc.
For the latest on Adobe Press books, go to www.adobepress.com.
To report errors, please send a note to errata@peachpit.com. For information regarding permissions, request forms and the appropriate contacts within the Pearson Education Global Rights & Permissions department, please visit www.pearsoned.com/permissions/.

Adobe Press Editor: Laura Norman	**Proofreader:** Kim Wimpsett
Development Editor: Victor Gavenda	**Compositor:** Kim Scott, Bumpy Design
Technical Reviewer: Jean-Claude Tremblay	**Indexer:** Valerie Haynes Perry
Senior Production Editor: Tracey Croom	**Cover & Interior Design:** Mimi Heft
Production Editor: Becky Winter	**Cover Illustration:** Axako/ShutterStock
Copyeditor: Liz Welch	

ISBN-13: 978-0-13-487838-6
ISBN–10:   0-13-487838-8

1 18

I'd like to dedicate this book to my wife Rebecca, my son Gabe, and my daughter Claire, who are the forces that drive me to do what I do every day. Thanks for putting up with me tapping away on my computer, especially early in the morning while we're on vacation. I'd also like to dedicate this to my Mom and Dad, who instilled in me that hard work always pays off. Finally, to all of my colleagues who are too numerous to mention but you know who you are and you all continue to inspire me every day.

About the Authors

Chad Chelius is a trainer, author, consultant, and speaker residing in the Philadelphia area. He's been using Adobe products for more than 25 years and began his career in the design and publishing industry.

An Adobe Certified Instructor and a consultant, he teaches and advises on all Adobe print and web products, specializing in InDesign and InCopy workflows, Illustrator, and PDF accessibility using Adobe Acrobat. He works with clients both large and small within and outside the United States, helping them to solve problems, to work smarter, and to work more efficiently using Adobe products.

Chad has been authoring content on Adobe products and related technologies for more than 15 years. He's worked with leading publishers such as Peachpit Press/ Adobe Press, Pearson Education, lynda.com, and LinkedIn Learning. He also contributes to *InDesign Magazine*, InDesignSecrets.com, InCopySecrets.com, and CreativePro.com.

As a speaker, Chad gives talks on Adobe applications at industry conferences of all sizes, including Adobe MAX, CreativePro Conference, The InDesign Conference, PepCon, and MakingDesign.

When he's not consulting and traveling, you'll find Chad hanging out with his family or riding his road bike in the hills of beautiful Pennsylvania or backpacking with his son. You can follow him on Twitter @chadchelius.

Rob Schwartz (author of Chapters 7 and 8) is an award-winning teacher with 20 years of experience in technical education. In addition to holding several Adobe Certified Associate certifications, Rob is an Adobe Certified Instructor. As an Adobe Education Leader, Rob won the prestigious Impact Award from Adobe, and in 2010 he ran the Top Certifying Academic Center for the Adobe certification exams and was named #1 Instructor Worldwide in the Adobe Certified Associate World Championship. Rob gives presentations worldwide about Adobe certifications.

Find out more about Rob at his online curriculum website: *brainbuffet.com*.

Contents

Getting Started

Welcome to *Learn Adobe Illustrator CC for Graphic Design and Illustration, Second Edition*! We use a combination of text and video to help you learn the basics of working in Adobe Illustrator CC. We introduce you to each skill in the context of a hands-on project. Be sure to watch the video and download the lesson files to follow along. In addition, we cover other areas that you will need to master to work as a graphic designer or illustrator, including how to work with clients and how to approach design.

About This Product

Learn Adobe Illustrator CC for Graphic Design and Illustration was created by a team of expert instructors, writers, and editors with years of experience in helping beginning learners get their start with the cool creative tools from Adobe. Our aim is not only to teach you the basics of the art of graphic design and illustration with Illustrator but to give you an introduction to the associated skills (like design principles and project management) that you'll need for your first job.

We've built the training around the objectives for the Graphic Design and Illustration Using Adobe Illustrator CC (2018) Adobe Certified Associate Exam. If you master the topics covered in this book and video, you'll be in good shape to take the exam. But even if certification isn't your goal, you'll still find this training will give you an excellent foundation for your future work in visual design. To that end, we've structured the material in the order that makes the most sense for beginning learners (as determined by experienced classroom teachers), rather than following the more arbitrary grouping of topics in the ACA Objectives.

To aid you in your quest, we've created a unique learning system that uses video and text in partnership. You'll experience this partnership in action in the Web Edition, which lives on your Account page at peachpit.com. The Web Edition contains 8 hours of video—the heart of the training—embedded in an online eBook that supports the video training and provides background material. The eBook material is also available separately for offline reading as a printed book or an eBook in a variety of formats. The Web Edition also includes hundreds of interactive review questions you can use to evaluate your progress. Purchase of the book in any format entitles you to free access to the Web Edition (instructions for accessing it follow later in this section).

Most chapters provide step-by-step instructions for creating a specific project or learning a specific technique. Many chapters include several optional tasks that let you further explore the features you've already learned. Chapters 7 and 8 acquaint you with other skills and concepts that you'll come to depend on as you use the software in your everyday work. Here is where you'll find most of the coverage of Domain 1 of the ACA Objectives, which don't specifically relate to features of Illustrator but are important components of the complete skill set that the ACA exam seeks to evaluate.

Each chapter opens with two lists of objectives. One list lays out the learning objectives: the specific tasks you'll learn in the chapter. The second list shows the ACA exam objectives that are covered in the chapter. A table at the end of the book guides you to coverage of all the exam objectives in the book or video.

Conventions Used in This Book

This book uses several elements styled in ways to help you as you work through the exercises.

Text that you should enter appears in bold, such as:

> With the guide still selected, enter **+.125** to the right of the current value of the X field in the Transform panel.

Terms that are defined in the Glossary appear in bold and in color, such as:

▶ **Video 2.3**
Adding Guides to a Document

> In Illustrator CC, you use the drawing tools on the Tools panel to create shapes.

Links to videos that cover the topics in depth appear in the margins.

★ *ACA Objective 2.1*

The ACA Objectives covered in the chapters are called out in the margins beside the sections that address them.

Notes give additional information about a topic. The information they contain is not essential to accomplishing a task but provides a more in-depth understanding of the topic.

> **NOTE**
>
> *After adding type on a path, you may want the type oriented to the other side of the path. To flip the type across the path, use the Selection tool to drag the middle bracket across the path.*

Operating System Differences

In most cases, Illustrator works the same in both Windows and macOS. Minor platform-specific differences do exist between the two versions, such as keyboard shortcuts, how dialog boxes are displayed, and how buttons are labeled. In most cases, screenshots were made in the Mac version of Illustrator and may appear somewhat differently from your own screen.

Where specific commands differ, they are noted within the text as follows:

Save your progress by pressing Command+S (macOS) or Ctrl+S (Windows).

In general, the Windows Ctrl key is equivalent to the Command key in macOS, and the Windows Alt key is equivalent to the Option key in macOS.

As lessons proceed, instructions may be truncated or shortened to save space, with the assumption that you picked up the essential concepts earlier in the lesson. For example, at the beginning of a lesson you may be instructed to "press Command+C (macOS) or Ctrl+C (Windows)." Later, you may be told to "copy" text or a graphic element. These should be considered identical instructions.

If you find you have difficulties in any particular task, review earlier steps or exercises in that lesson. In some cases, if an exercise is based on concepts covered earlier, you will be referred to the specific lesson.

Installing the Software

Before you begin using *Learn Adobe Illustrator CC for Graphic Design and Illustration*, make sure that your system is set up correctly and that you've installed the proper software and hardware. This material is based on the original 2018 release of Adobe Illustrator CC (version 22) and is designed to cover the objectives of the Adobe Certified Associate Exam for that version of the software.

The Adobe Illustrator CC software is not included with this book; it is available only with an Adobe Creative Cloud membership, which you must purchase, or it must be supplied by your school or other organization. In addition to Adobe Illustrator CC, some lessons in this book have steps that can be performed with Adobe Bridge CC and other Adobe applications or web services such as Typekit. You must install these applications from Adobe Creative Cloud onto your computer. Follow the instructions provided at *helpx.adobe.com/creative-cloud/help/ download-install-app.html*.

ADOBE CREATIVE CLOUD DESKTOP APP

In addition to Adobe Illustrator CC, this training requires the Adobe Creative Cloud desktop application, which provides a central location for managing the dozens of apps and services that are included in a Creative Cloud membership. You can use the Creative Cloud desktop application to sync and share files, manage fonts, access libraries of stock photography and design assets, and showcase and discover creative work in the design community.

The Creative Cloud desktop application is installed automatically when you download your first Creative Cloud product. If you have Adobe Application Manager installed, it auto-updates to the Creative Cloud desktop application.

If the Creative Cloud desktop application is not installed on your computer, you can download it from the Download Creative Cloud page on the Adobe website (*creative.adobe.com/products/creative-cloud*) or the Adobe Creative Cloud desktop apps page (*www.adobe.com/creativecloud/catalog/desktop.html*). If you are using software on classroom machines, be sure to check with your instructor before making any changes to the installed software or system configuration.

CHECKING FOR UPDATES

Adobe periodically provides updates to software. You can easily obtain these updates through the Creative Cloud. If these updates include new features that affect the content of this training or the objectives of the ACA exam in any way, we will post updated material to peachpit.com.

Accessing the Free Web Edition and Lesson Files

Your purchase of this product in any format includes access to the corresponding Web Edition hosted on peachpit.com. The Web Edition contains the complete text of the book augmented with hours of video and interactive quizzes.

TIP

You'll find a video walkthrough of these instructions at www.peachpit.com/ LearnACAillustrator.

If you purchased an eBook from peachpit.com or adobepress.com, the Web Edition will automatically appear on the Digital Purchases tab on your Account page. Click the Launch link to access the product.

Continue reading to learn how to register your product to get access to the lesson files.

If you purchased an eBook from a different vendor or you bought a print book, you must register your purchase on peachpit.com:

1　Go to *www.peachpit.com/register*.

2　Sign in or create a new account.

3　Enter ISBN: **9780134878386**.

4　Answer the questions as proof of purchase.

5　The Web Edition will appear under the Digital Purchases tab on your Account page. Click the Launch link to access the product.

To work through the projects in this product, you will first need to download the lesson files from peachpit.com. You can download the files for individual lessons or download them all in a single file.

The Lesson Files can be accessed through the Registered Products tab on your Account page. Click the Access Bonus Content link below the title of your product to proceed to the download page. Click the lesson file links to download them to your computer.

Project Fonts

All fonts used in these projects are either part of standard system installs or can be downloaded from Typekit, an Adobe web service that is included with your Creative Cloud membership. If you don't have the fonts mentioned in the video, you can install them or explore the fonts you have available on your system if this is not an option.

Additional Resources

Learn Adobe Illustrator CC for Graphic Design and Illustration is not meant to replace documentation that comes with the program or to be a comprehensive reference for every feature. For comprehensive information about program features and tutorials, refer to these resources:

Adobe Illustrator CC Learn & Support: *helpx.adobe.com/illustrator.html* is where you can find and browse Help and Support content on Adobe.com. Adobe Illustrator Learn & Support are accessible from the Help menu in Illustrator. Help is also available as a printable PDF document. Download the document at *https://helpx.adobe.com/pdf/illustrator_reference.pdf.*

Adobe Forums: *forums.adobe.com/community/illustrator* lets you tap into peer-to-peer discussions, questions, and answers on Adobe products.

Adobe Illustrator CC product home page: *adobe.com/products/illustrator* provides information about new features and intuitive ways to create professional-quality videos that play back on a wide range of devices.

Adobe Exchange: *www.adobeexchange.com* is a central resource for finding tools, services, extensions, code samples, and more to supplement and extend your Adobe products.

Resources for educators: *adobe.com/education* and *edex.adobe.com* offer a treasure trove of information for instructors who teach classes on Adobe software at all levels.

Adobe Certification

The Adobe training and certification programs are designed to help video editors, designers, and other creative professionals improve and promote their product-proficiency skills. The Adobe Certified Associate (ACA) is an industry-recognized credential that demonstrates proficiency in Adobe digital skills. Whether you're just starting out in your career, looking to switch jobs, or interested in preparing students for success in the job market, the Adobe Certified Associate program is for you! For more information visit *edex.adobe.com/aca*.

Resetting the Preferences to Their Default Settings

Illustrator lets you determine how the program looks and behaves (like tool settings and the default unit of measurement) using the extensive options in Edit > Preferences (Windows) or Illustrator CC > Preferences (macOS). To ensure that the preferences and default settings of your Adobe Illustrator program match those used in this book, you can reset your preference settings to their defaults. If you are using software installed on computers in a classroom, don't make any changes to the system configuration without first checking with your instructor.

To reset your preferences to their default settings, follow these steps:

1 Quit Illustrator.

2 Hold down the Cmd+Option+Shift keys (macOS) or Ctrl+Alt+Shift keys (Windows).

3 Continue to hold the keys and start Adobe Illustrator CC.

   When Illustrator finishes launching, you'll see that your Preferences settings have been reset to their default values.

CHAPTER OBJECTIVES

Chapter Learning Objectives

- Open, create, save, and export files.
- Understand the difference between raster and vector artwork.
- Become familiar with the Adobe Illustrator CC interface.
- Work with panels in Illustrator.
- Use, create, and save workspaces.

Chapter ACA Objectives

For full descriptions of the objectives, see the table on pages 196–204.

DOMAIN 1.0
WORKING IN THE DESIGN INDUSTRY
1.1, 1.4, 1.4a, 1.4b

DOMAIN 2.0
PROJECT SETUP AND INTERFACE
2.1, 2.2

DOMAIN 5.0
PUBLISHING DIGITAL MEDIA
5.2

CHAPTER 1

Introduction to Adobe Illustrator CC 2018

You are about to learn how to use one of the most powerful and flexible illustration programs available on the market today. A wide range of designers and artists use Adobe Illustrator CC to create a variety of types of electronic artwork.

You see artwork created in Adobe Illustrator every day in brochures, on business cards, in flyers, in catalogs, and in product illustrations, just to name a few. Probably the most common type of content created in Illustrator is logos. Almost every logo you see on a daily basis was created in Adobe Illustrator thanks to the power and flexibility that Illustrator provides to designers and artists all over the globe.

Careers that involve the use of Illustrator range from fine artists to graphic designers to illustrators to technical artists—and everything in between. The need for designers and artists who are proficient in Illustrator spans many different industries, but the work they do in all of them is based on a common set of skills.

Learn Adobe Illustrator CC

As with all of the products in the Adobe Press Learn ACA series, one of the goals of this book and video combination is to give you a solid foundation in the set of skills you'll need to tackle your first professional projects in Adobe Illustrator CC. To accomplish that goal you don't need to know every tool and feature found in the program, but you do need to know which features are essential for taking an Illustrator project all the way from setup through layout and production and then to final printed or digital output.

When you're working on the projects in this book, you have the freedom to explore and make your projects your own. You're certainly welcome to follow along with my examples, but please feel free to change text or styles to fit your own interests. After all, you'll need to come up with your own ideas and content in the real world! When you're sure you grasp the concepts I'm talking about, I encourage you to apply them in your own way. In some projects, you may want to even take things beyond the scope of what appears in the book and videos. Make these projects your own!

Prepare for the ACA Exam

This book and its accompanying video cover every objective for the Adobe Certified Associate (ACA) exam, but I won't discuss them in numerical order. Instead, I focus on showing you how to build design projects, and along the way I'll cover the objectives as I deem appropriate. The authors of this series are teachers and trainers, and we've been doing this for a long time. We'll cover the concepts in the order that makes the most sense for *learning* and *retaining* the information. You'll read everything you need to pass the exam and qualify for an entry-level job—but don't focus on that now. Instead, focus on having a blast learning Adobe Illustrator!

Launching Adobe Illustrator CC

To get started, you need to launch Adobe Illustrator CC. You can do so in a number of different ways depending on the computer platform you are using (macOS or Windows).

To launch Adobe Illustrator in macOS, do one of the following:

- Locate the application in the Applications folder and double-click the application icon.
- Launch the application from the Creative Cloud desktop application found in the menu bar (MacOS) or the task pane (Windows).
- Perform a search using the Spotlight feature, which can be accessed by clicking the Spotlight icon Q in the menu bar of your computer. Simply type **Illustrator** in the search field and Spotlight should locate the application.
- If you add the Adobe Illustrator CC application icon to the dock, you can also launch the application by clicking the icon.

To launch Adobe Illustrator on a Windows computer, do one of the following:

- Locate the application in your Program Files folder on your computer and double-click the application icon.
- Perform a search by clicking the Windows Start icon and typing **Illustrator** in the search field, and Windows should locate the application.
- You can also add Adobe Illustrator CC to the task bar by pinning it permanently to the task bar for easy access in the future.

What Is Adobe Illustrator CC?

★ *ACA Objective 1.4a*

 *Video 1.1*
*What Is Adobe
Illustrator CC?*

In the simplest terms, Adobe Illustrator is a vector-based drawing and illustration application. *Vector-based* refers to the method that Adobe Illustrator uses to draw, generate, and display shapes. These vector objects are mathematically generated paths that can be scaled and adjusted without any ill effects on the artwork. Don't worry—you don't need to be a math wizard to use Illustrator! Illustrator does all of the calculations for you automatically.

This is important because it allows the user to scale and manipulate artwork infinitely. For example, let's say you have a 3" x 3" logo and need to scale it up to use on a huge outdoor banner for an upcoming event. Illustrator lets you do this because it draws the banner using vector graphics rather than as a grid of pixels. When you think vectors, think wireframes that can be manipulated and sized to any required dimension.

Raster-based (pixel-based) artwork contrasts significantly from Illustrator in that it has a specific resolution tied to it that limits the amount that you can resize it (**Figure 1.1**). Adobe Photoshop is generally the tool of choice used by designers to open and manipulate raster-based artwork. At some point during a designer's journey, they may grab a logo from a website and attempt to use it in the design of a brochure. Only after printing out the brochure do they realize that the logo looks horrible because the logo was pixel based and the resolution that was sufficient for a website is now insufficient for use in a printed brochure. Live and learn!

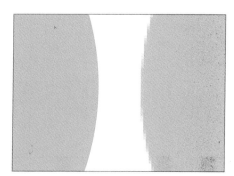

Figure 1.1 Vector artwork (left) contains crisp, clean lines even when the artwork is magnified. Raster artwork (right) is made up of pixels and has a specific resolution tied to that file that limits its use in some instances.

That's not to say that raster-based artwork doesn't come into play when working in Illustrator. Your design might call for *raster effects* such as drop shadows and outer glows. These effects will be converted from vector art to bitmap art, or rasterized, when the file is output. The Raster Effects setting for each document determines the resolution of the bitmap that will be generated. Another word sometimes used for rasterizing is rendering.

Now make no mistake; there is a time and a place for raster-based artwork. Digital photographs are a great example. The sort of detail and subtle shading that distinguish photographs can be reproduced only as raster art. The point is to use the correct type of file for your project's needs.

★ *ACA Objective 2.2*

An Overview of the Adobe Illustrator Interface

▶ **Video 1.2** *An Overview of the Adobe Illustrator CC Interface*

To be proficient in Adobe Illustrator, you need to become comfortable with the working environment. This chapter will help you to get acquainted with the numerous tools and panels that you'll be using in the projects you'll be building.

Opening a File

When you first launch Adobe Illustrator CC, you'll be presented with the Start workspace by default (**Figure 1.2**). We'll talk about workspaces in a bit, but for now simply understand that a workspace is a specific configuration of the Illustrator interface. The Start workspace is quite minimal, especially at this point where you may not have any recent files to display. The Start workspace is relatively new to Illustrator CC. If you decide that you don't like the Start workspace and would prefer that it didn't display each time a file is closed or when you initially launch Illustrator, you can disable this option by choosing Illustrator CC > Preferences (macOS) or Edit > Preferences (Windows) and deselecting Show The Start Workspace When No Documents Are Open in the General category of the Preferences dialog box.

On the left side of the screen you'll notice the Open and Create New buttons. Clicking Open (as you might expect) opens a file, equivalent to choosing File > Open. The more you work in Adobe Illustrator CC and the more files you open and create, the more content you'll see in this Start workspace after you initially launch Illustrator.

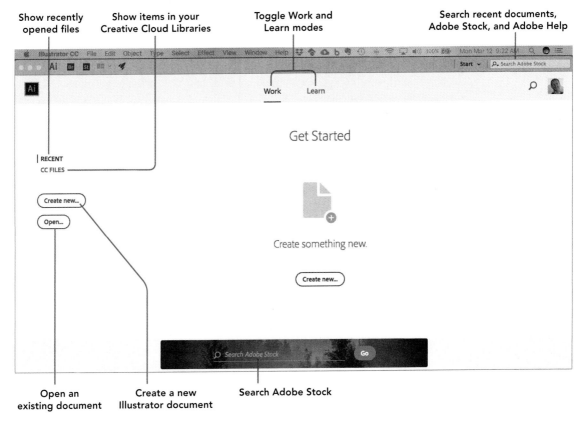

Show recently opened files

Show items in your Creative Cloud Libraries

Toggle Work and Learn modes

Search recent documents, Adobe Stock, and Adobe Help

Open an existing document

Create a new Illustrator document

Search Adobe Stock

Figure 1.2 The Start workspace in Adobe Illustrator

If you're just getting started with Illustrator and need some inspiration, you can use the Search Adobe Stock field at the bottom of the Start workspace to look for stock photos, illustrations, and artwork that you can purchase (some is available for free) and use as a basis for your artwork. Once you've worked with Illustrator for a while, you may have some files stored in your Creative Cloud Libraries for sharing with other Adobe applications or for collaborating with other workers. For now, click the Open button and navigate to the lesson files for this lesson. Open the `01_01_face.ai` file and click OK.

If the Missing Fonts dialog box opens, you can activate the fonts if you have them available, or simply click the Close button to dismiss the dialog box. We'll discuss fonts in more detail in a future lesson.

Elements of the Adobe Illustrator Interface

As soon as you open a file in Illustrator, the workspace will change from the Start workspace to the Essentials workspace by default. The first things you'll see at the very top of your screen are the menu bar and the Application bar (**Figure 1.3**). This is one area where you could see a discrepancy between the macOS and Windows platforms. On macOS, the menu bar is a separate element that appears above the Application bar, but on Windows, the menu bar is merged with the Application bar. Also, the macOS platform gives you the ability to turn the Application bar on and off. To do this, first disable the Application frame by choosing Window > Application Frame; then you can hide the Application bar by choosing Window > Application Bar. The Windows platform doesn't give you the ability to hide the Application frame or Application bar.

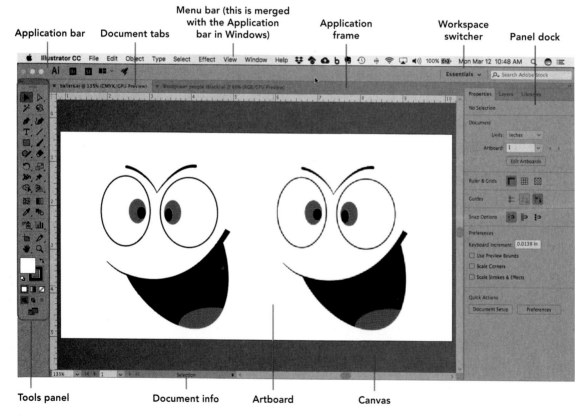

Figure 1.3 The many pieces of the Illustrator interface

To the right of the Application bar, you have the Workspace switcher menu, which allows you to change the appearance and locations of panels in Illustrator to the predefined setup defined in each workspace. You can create your own custom workspaces as you see fit.

When you open one or more documents, provided that the Application frame is currently enabled, each document will open in its own tab within one Document window. This allows you to easily switch the view to a different document and even view several documents at the same time by using the arrange icon found in the Application bar.

As mentioned earlier, both the macOS and Windows versions of Illustrator contain an Application frame, which is the overall container that holds all of the elements of the Illustrator interface. The macOS version of Adobe Illustrator CC provides a means by which you can disable the Application frame and in turn the Application bar should you choose to. With the Application frame disabled, all of your document windows "float" independently of the Illustrator interface; however, they may be consolidated as tabs depending on the settings you've chosen in Preferences.

The Tools panel, which is on the left side of the Adobe Illustrator interface, displays each and every tool available within Illustrator. This panel can be displayed in a two-column mode or a single-column mode by clicking the ▦ icon in the upper-left corner of the Tools panel.

The panel dock is on the right side of the Illustrator interface. As part of the Essentials workspace, it contains three panels by default: the Properties panel, the Layers panel, and the Libraries panel. The Properties panel is new in Adobe Illustrator CC 2018 and is designed to include commonly used options in one convenient location as opposed to you having to open multiple panels to perform the same action. As a beginning Illustrator user, you'll find a lot of the options that you need right there in the Properties panel.

You'll notice that the Properties panel is contextual. What I mean is that based on the object that you have selected, the Properties panel will show you options and choices related to that particular object. For example, if you select an object, it will show you the fill, stroke, and positioning options for that object. If you select text, the Properties panel will show you the font menu, type size (measured in points), leading, and more related to options available for formatting type.

The artboard is where the artwork for your project lives. You can think of the artboard like a piece of paper. The artwork that you actually want to appear in your project and that you'll use as part of the project should be placed directly on the artboard. Keeping your artwork on the artboard also gives you more control when placing an Illustrator file into other Adobe applications such as InDesign and Photoshop.

The canvas is a working area within an Illustrator file. Anything outside the bounds of the artboard is considered the canvas and is often used by artists and designers as a "working" area to experiment or store elements that they might need later on during the design process.

At the very bottom of the Illustrator interface, you'll see the Document Info section. This displays the current zoom level at which you're viewing the artwork and allows you to change the zoom level by clicking the arrow to its right and choosing a new zoom value from the menu. You can also navigate to different artboards should your document contain more than one, and it also displays information about the currently selected tool (by default). You can click the arrow to the right of that area to change what is displayed while working in Illustrator.

★ ACA Objective 1.1

★ ACA Objective 2.1

Creating a New Document

When beginning a document from scratch in Illustrator, you'll need to create a new document in which to work. This can be done from the Start workspace in Illustrator by clicking the Create New button. You can also access this feature by choosing File > New. This displays the New Document dialog box.

Within the New Document dialog box, you'll need to make some choices that will depend on the project you plan on creating. These choices will be based on discussions with the client and project goals that have been established before work has begun. You'll want to keep in mind who your audience is, what their needs are, and, more important, what their goals are. Establishing these items before you even begin working will help you create a successful project.

The New Document dialog box is divided into five categories that can be seen along the top of the dialog box. These categories are as follows:

- **Mobile:** Used for creating artwork intended for mobile devices. Common mobile device sizes are provided to aid you in creating artwork at the correct size and dimensions for various mobile devices. This type of document uses the pixel unit of measurement and the RGB document color mode by default.

- **Web:** Used for creating comps and mock-ups for websites. Illustrator is a great prototyping tool for creating the initial design for web pages. Although Illustrator won't code the web pages for you, it will provide you with some powerful features to assist in the process. This type of document uses the pixel unit of measurement and the RGB color mode by default.

- **Print:** Used for creating print-based documents such as logos and other artwork destined for print output and contains common print paper sizes to get you started. This type of document uses points as the unit of measurement and the CMYK color mode by default.

- **Film & Video:** That's right; although Illustrator can't edit video, it's common to create artwork in Illustrator that will be used in video projects. Creating a document from this category will provide video-safe areas as guides to ensure that text and graphic elements placed in a video project will not get cut off when displayed on a TV or monitor with older aspect ratios (4:5 vs. 16:9). This type of document uses pixels as the unit of measurement and the RGB color mode by default.

- **Art & Illustration:** Used for creating various types of art and illustration documents at various sizes such as a poster. This type of document uses points as the unit of measurement and the RGB color mode by default.

Customizing Document Settings

★ *ACA Objective 1.4b*

Regardless of which preset you start with, these are just jumping-off points for creating a new document. After choosing a preset, you can customize the properties to the right of the dialog box to match the requirements of the project (**Figure 1.4**). This is a common practice since the presets often don't have exactly the right properties that you need.

In this section you can change the unit of measurement to the one that you prefer to work with. I personally don't find points of much value when creating a print document, so I changed the unit of measurement to inches. You can then customize the width and height of the document along with the orientation by clicking either the landscape or portrait icons. You can also define the number of artboards that you want to use in your project. For example, you might already know that you need to provide the client with three different options of a logo from which they can choose. In that case, you can specify three artboards in the New Document dialog box. It's important not to think of Illustrator artboards as pages; think of them as individual elements or versions for your project. Illustrator is not a page layout tool—that would be a job for Adobe InDesign.

Figure 1.4 Specifying properties in the New Document dialog box

Next you can define the amount of bleed for your project. Bleed is applicable only to print projects in which the design will extend all the way to the edge of the paper. Let's say you're designing a business card and you have elements that are intended to be printed all the way to the edge of the paper. To achieve this end result, you'd set Bleed values (distances) for each edge of your document in the New Document dialog box. Then, when creating your artwork, you'd extend the artwork past the edge of the artboard to the bleed guide. Bleed is used to overcome the limitations of the printing process, and it's important that you build your documents correctly to help you achieve the desired goal without encountering unnecessary problems along the way.

CMYK is chosen from the Color Mode menu for a print project by default, and this is generally a good choice for printing. This means that the colors will be created by mixing cyan, magenta, yellow, and black inks, a method known as process color. It's always a good idea, however, to have a discussion with your printer to ensure that no problems are encountered later on in the production process.

You'll notice that the Raster Effects settings are set to 300 ppi, which is high resolution for print output. This would come into play if you use any raster-based effects in an Illustrator document.

Finally, the Preview Mode menu is set to Default, which will display your artwork as it will appear when printed. Other Preview Mode choices include Pixel for web and mobile artwork, and Overprint to help you see how elements will overprint in your document should those elements exist. Once you've customized the values in the New Document dialog box, click OK to create the new document.

Changing Document Properties

Once you create a document, you can display helpful properties right in the Properties panel that will make it easier for you to work inside Illustrator. Sometimes, regardless of how much preplanning you do, you'll realize that you need to make adjustments. Let's take a closer look at how to do that.

With the new document open on your computer, look at the Properties panel at the right side of your screen (**Figure 1.5**). Keep in mind that we currently have nothing selected in the document. Therefore, the options that you currently see in the Properties panel are related to the settings of the document itself. At the top of the Properties panel, note that you can change the unit of measurement as well as navigate and edit the artboards in the document. Click the Edit Artboards button, and notice that there are now handles around every side and on every corner of the selected artboard (**Figure 1.6**). Also, the Artboard tool ⌐ has automatically been selected. Drag any handle of the artboard to resize it. When you're finished, click the Selection tool ▶ so that nothing is selected.

Figure 1.5 The options available in the Properties panel with no object selected

Figure 1.6 Editing the current artboard

TIP

To quickly deselect the current tool and select the ever-popular Selection tool, simply press the letter V on your keyboard. If you currently have the Type tool selected, you can press the Esc key to select the Selection tool.

Further down in the Properties panel, you'll see the Ruler & Grids section. Clicking the Show Rulers button ⌐ displays the rulers along the left and top of the document. Rulers help you to see the size of objects on the page and are also the primary method for creating guides in an Illustrator file. Clicking the Show Rulers button again will hide the rulers. The same behavior occurs when clicking the Show Grid ⊞ and Show Transparency Grid ▨ buttons in the Ruler & Grids section of the Properties panel. These buttons display the document grid (as defined in preferences) and the Transparency Grid, respectively.

The Guides section of the Properties panel makes managing guides easy. Simply click one of these buttons:

⊞ hides and shows guides.

⊞ locks and unlocks guides.

⊧ hides or shows Smart Guides.

These buttons behave like toggle switches. Click the button to enable the feature; click the button again to disable it.

The Preferences section of the Properties panel also provides quick access to common settings that users need to adjust frequently. Here you can change the keyboard increment when nudging objects, show or hide the preview bounds of objects, and control whether corners and strokes and effects should be scaled when transforming.

The far bottom of the Properties panel contains the Quick Actions section. Here you can click the Document Setup button to change the properties of the document. The Document Setup dialog box provides users with a way to adjust the size of the document and change the bleed settings, along with several other related features. If you click the Preferences button, you'll be taken to the Illustrator Preferences dialog box, where you can customize the behavior and appearance of the Illustrator application.

★ *ACA Objective 2.2*

▶ **Video 1.4**
Customizing the Workspace

Customizing the Workspace

To help you stay organized and to allow you to work on various types of documents, Illustrator contains several workspaces that are available for you to choose from. Earlier we talked about how the Start workspace is displayed when no documents are open in Illustrator and how that workspace automatically changes to the

Essentials workspace once you open or create a new document. Let's take a look at a few of the available workspaces.

1   Open the Workspace switcher to see the list of workspaces.

2   Choose Typography from the list. Note how the panels that are displayed in Illustrator change and possibly move or are hidden when that workspace is chosen.

3   Open the Workspace switcher again, and this time choose Tracing. Note once again that the panels that are displayed are quite different from the previous workspace that you had chosen.

The predefined workspaces in Illustrator are certainly helpful, but the reality is that each user works in a different way and more than likely works on different types of projects. The default workspaces may not lend themselves to every type of project that you'll be working on. Fortunately, we're not stuck with the workspaces that are provided in Illustrator—we can create our own!

Working with Panels

To accommodate the needs of all users, it's possible to configure the arrangement of the panels in Illustrator in an almost unlimited set of ways. So that we begin with our panels at a common location, choose Essentials Classic from the Workspace Switcher menu, and then from the same menu choose Reset Essentials Classic (**Figure 1.7**). This resets all the panels to the default location as defined in the Essentials Classic workspace.

Panel Behavior

Panels can appear in different states within Illustrator. A panel can be expanded, collapsed, or floating, depending on how the panel is being used and which behavior you prefer. Open the Window menu at the top of your screen. Note the options available under this menu. It's important to know that every panel in Illustrator lives in this menu. So if you ever have trouble finding a panel, simply open the Window menu and choose the panel that you'd like to display. For this example, choose Window > Navigator. If the panel is already saved in the current workspace, it will open wherever the panel is docked within that workspace. If it's not part of the current workspace, it will open as a floating panel, as is the case here.

Many of the panels in Illustrator can be resized, but the sizes of some are fixed. Choose Window > Align to open the Align panel. Hover your cursor over one of the

Figure 1.7 Choosing the Essentials Classic workspace and then resetting it to its default appearance

corners of the Navigator panel (**Figure 1.8**). Notice that your cursor changes to a scale icon, indicating that the panel can be resized. Now hover your cursor over one of the corners of the Align panel. Notice that the scale icon does not appear. That's because the Align panel is one of those panels that can't be scaled. Due to the content contained in that panel, there's no value in scaling that panel. The Navigator, on the other hand, is used to navigate a document and benefits from being scaled.

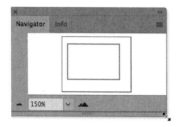
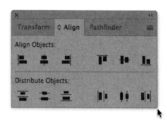

Figure 1.8 The Navigator panel (left) can be resized when you drag on one of the panel corners. The Align panel (right) is a fixed size and cannot be resized.

Both of the panels that we displayed are floating because they were not configured as part of the docked panels defined in the Essentials Classic workspace. When a panel is floating, it can be moved and repositioned anywhere on your screen. Use the small bar at the top of one of the panels to drag it to a new location (**Figure 1.9**). One of the downsides to floating panels is that they cover the artwork in your Illustrator document. I often see users spending more time moving panels out of the way than they do working on the document! We'll talk about ways to avoid this in a bit.

Figure 1.9 Dragging a panel group to reposition it

Note that when you displayed either the Navigator panel or the Align panel, other panels were displayed alongside. This is because each of those panels is part of a panel group.

Panels do not have to remain grouped with the panels that they're initially displayed with. You can ungroup them so that the panels are floating as individual panels. To ungroup a panel from a group of panels, drag it by its tab outside of the group to a new location (**Figure 1.10**).

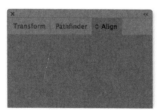
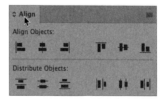

Figure 1.10 Removing a panel from a panel group

Conversely, you can group panels into any arrangement that you wish by reversing the previous process. Simply drag the tab of a panel on top of the tab area of another existing panel. A blue outline will appear showing the drop zone where the panel being dragged is going to be added (**Figure 1.11**). Release the mouse button and the panel is added to the group.

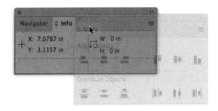

Figure 1.11 Adding a panel to a group

Panels can also be stacked. This process is similar to grouping except the panels are connected at the top and bottom instead of nested into tabs. To stack a panel, drag the tab or title bar of a panel onto the top or bottom of another existing panel or panel group. When a blue drop zone line appears, release the mouse button to stack the panel at the dropped location (**Figure 1.12**).

Floating panels and even panels that are docked but expanded can be minimized or maximized. To minimize a panel or panel group, simply double-click the tab or tab area (the area to the side of the tab). You'll notice that the contents of the panel disappear, showing only the tabs at the top. To maximize, simply double-click the tab or tab area again (**Figure 1.13**).

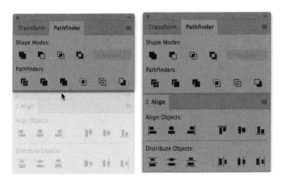

Figure 1.13 Minimized panels (above); maximized panels (right)

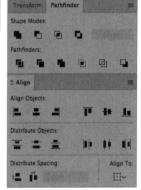

Figure 1.12 Dragging a panel and stacking it with another panel (left); the result (right)

Docking Panels

A more efficient approach to panel management is to dock the panels. Docking panels organizes the panels on either the left or right side of the screen and keeps the panels out of the way of your document while you're working. Docked panels don't cover up any of your artwork until you decide to use one of the panels.

To dock a panel, drag the tab if you only want to dock a single panel, or drag the title bar if you want to dock a group of panels, and drag to the right side of your screen where the panel dock is located. When you see a blue drop zone, release the mouse to dock the panel at that location. Note that if you see a horizontal blue drop zone, you're going to dock the panel(s) with existing panels. If you see a vertical drop zone, you'll create a new column of panels in the panel dock (**Figure 1.14**).

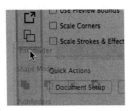

Figure 1.14 If you see a horizontal blue drop zone, you're adding a panel to an existing column of panels (left). If you see a vertical blue drop zone, you're creating a new column of panels.

It's important to understand that panels can be docked on both the right side of the Illustrator interface, where many panels are docked already, and on the left side of the Illustrator interface, right next to the Tools panel.

Once a panel is docked, the panel can be collapsed to icon mode or it can be in expanded mode. If you look at the Essentials Classic workspace that you loaded earlier in this lesson, you'll notice that the Properties panel and Libraries panel are expanded. This means that even though the panels are docked, you can see all of the options available in that panel at all times.

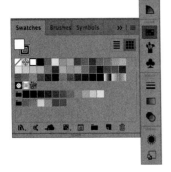

To the left of the Properties panel, you'll see several icons stacked on top of one another in a vertical column. These panels are collapsed into icons. The advantage of panels collapsed into icons is that the icons occupy very little screen real estate until you're ready to use the panels. If you click one of the icons, you'll see the full panel displayed next to the icon. Think of these icons as toggle switches. Click the icon to display the panel; then use the panel options and click the icon again to close the panel (**Figure 1.15**).

The icons aren't always easy to figure out when you're trying to find a specific panel. To make it easier to see which panel is which, drag the left edge of the column of icons to the left to make the icons a little bigger so that you can also see the name of the icon (**Figure 1.16**). This will help you to find the panel you want to use faster and more easily.

Figure 1.15 Clicking a panel icon displays the full panel next to the icon. Clicking the icon again closes the panel.

Figure 1.16 Opening up the column of docked collapsed icons to see the name of each panel

Figure 1.17 The Properties and Libraries panels in expanded mode (left), and the same panels collapsed to icons (right)

Figure 1.18 The Swatches panel with the panel menu displayed

Once a panel is docked, you can expand or collapse the panels by clicking the double-arrow icon located in the upper-right corner of the dock. When the double-arrow icon is pointing to the left, it indicates that the panels in that dock are collapsed, and when the double-arrow icon is pointing to the right, it indicates that the panels in that dock are expanded (**Figure 1.17**). Go ahead and try it for yourself! This icon is also like a toggle switch. Click the icon to expand or collapse the panels, and click the icon again to reverse it.

Panel Menus

With very few exceptions, every panel in Illustrator also contains a panel menu ▤. Panel menus list options related to the panel in which you are working (**Figure 1.18**). If each panel showed every possible option within the panel itself, each panel would be quite large. So instead, the most commonly used options are displayed in the panel, and additional options are found in the panel menu.

Showing Panel Options

Some panels provide an option to show a bare minimum set of choices within the panel. You'll know if more options are available by the presence of an up- and down-arrow icon 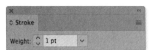 to the left of the panel name. Clicking this icon will toggle between the minimum and maximum amount of options displayed in the panel. Some panels even offer a state showing no options at all. To take one example, open the Stroke panel. Clicking the up- and down-arrow icon will show you minimal options, a medium amount of options, and then the maximum amount of options (**Figure 1.19**). These options can also be toggled by choosing Show Options or Hide Options from the panel menu, respectively.

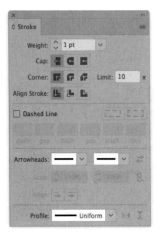

Figure 1.19 The Stroke panel with the minimum number of options displayed (above) and with the maximum number of options displayed (right)

Saving a Workspace

Figure 1.20 Creating a new workspace

Once you've configured your panels so they support the way that you like to work, it's a good idea to save that configuration so that you can always go back to that saved state at any time. The panel configuration is saved by using a workspace. Think of a workspace as your working environment, just like your desk. Some people have a clean and tidy desk; others might have a very messy desk. The point here is that Illustrator lets you work the way that you prefer. The difference is that with a workspace you can clean it up and reset it at any time. I wish I could do the same to my desk!

To create a new workspace, open the Workspace switcher menu in the upper-right corner of your screen and choose New Workspace (**Figure 1.20**).

In the New Workspace dialog box, enter a unique and memorable name for your workspace. In this example, I called my workspace **My Tidy Workspace** (**Figure 1.21**). Click OK.

Now that the workspace is created, you'll find it listed on the Workspace switcher menu at the top of the Illustrator interface. If you ever want to make an update to your workspace, simply adjust the panels in a new configuration, choose New Workspace from the Workspace switcher menu, and in the New Workspace dialog box give the workspace the same name as the old one. You'll see a warning that if you click OK, you'll overwrite the old one. Click OK to replace the old one.

If you ever want to delete a workspace that you no longer need, you can do so by choosing Manage Workspaces from the Workspace switcher menu to open the Manage Workspaces dialog box (**Figure 1.22**). Here you can delete any unwanted workspaces (by selecting them and clicking the trash can icon) and add new ones (by clicking the New Workspace button) if you wish.

Figure 1.21 Naming and saving a workspace

Figure 1.22 Managing workspaces

Saving and Exporting Files

★ *ACA Objective 5.2*

▶ **Video 1.4** *Saving and Exporting Documents*

Illustrator gives users the ability to save files in a number of different formats for use in various situations. For typical graphic design situations, the Adobe Illustrator format (`.ai`) is the format of choice. There will be cases, however, when you'll need to save an Illustrator document to a different format to meet the needs of the project.

With a file open in Illustrator, choose File > Save As or simply File > Save if this is the first time you're saving the document. The Save As dialog box opens

(**Figure 1.23**); here you can choose where to save your file as well as the name you'd like to give the file. More important, at the bottom of the dialog box, you'll find the Save As Type menu (Windows) or the Format menu (macOS), where you can choose the format in which you want to save the file. Adobe Illustrator CC provides six file format options.

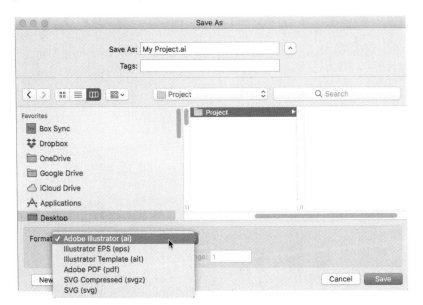

- **Adobe Illustrator (.ai):** This is the native file format of Illustrator and requires that users have Illustrator installed on their computer in order to open the file. This format can be placed in page layout applications such as Adobe InDesign.

- **Illustrator EPS (.eps):** This saves the file as an Encapsulated PostScript File and can be opened in Illustrator as well as other compatible editors. This format can also be placed in other page layout applications such as Adobe InDesign.

- **Illustrator Template (.ait):** This format is useful for creating template files that contain foundational elements such as swatches, styles, and graphic styles that will serve as the foundation for other designs with similar appearances.

- **Adobe PDF (.pdf):** The Portable Document Format is used for sharing files with a wide range of users. A file saved in the PDF format can be opened by anyone using Adobe Acrobat or the free Adobe Acrobat Reader.

- **SVG Compressed (.svgz):** The SVG (Scalable Vector Graphic) format is a web-based vector format often used for creating responsive web designs. This flavor of SVG is a compressed version.

- **SVG (.svg):** The SVG (Scalable Vector Graphic) format is a web-based vector format often used for creating responsive web designs.

Choose Adobe Illustrator from the menu and click Save. In the Illustrator Options dialog box that opens (**Figure 1.24**), you can choose the settings for saving the file. The Version menu gives users the ability to save a document to be opened in older versions of Adobe Illustrator. If you're not concerned with opening this file in older versions, leave the choice set to Illustrator CC. Illustrator will embed the necessary font characters used in the document provided the licensing for the font allows it. This doesn't mean that you won't need the font when opening the file, but if the file is placed in another application, the fonts will be included. If you don't need the entire font file to be embedded in the document, use the field in the Fonts section to tell Illustrator when to embed a portion of the font. It's always a good idea to enable the Create PDF Compatible File check box to ensure that this file can be placed in other applications. The default settings are typically sufficient for most applications. Click OK to save the document.

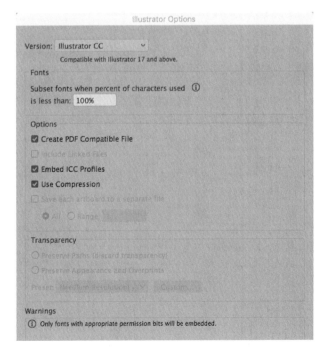

Figure 1.24 The Illustrator Options dialog box provides options for controlling how the Illustrator file is saved.

In addition to the options available when saving a document, there are even more options available when exporting a file. Illustrator generally reserves the Save As function for the vector-based formats and the Export function for raster-based formats, but you'll notice some overlap between the two. To export a file, choose File > Export > Export As. The Export dialog box opens (**Figure 1.25**).

In the Save As Type menu (Windows) or the Format menu (macOS), you'll see all of the available export formats. Most of these formats are raster- or pixel-based formats; however, there are some unique formats available such as CSS, Flash, and Text. We're not going to discuss all of these formats here, but simply know that when you need to convert your Illustrator artwork to a different format, the Export command is what you'll want to use.

Figure 1.25 The Export command provides the ability to export an Illustrator file to a wide range of formats.

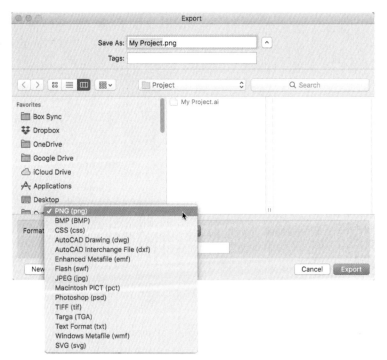

CHAPTER OBJECTIVES

Chapter Learning Objectives

- Create a new document and choose document settings.
- Set preferences in Adobe Illustrator CC.
- Add guides to an Illustrator document.
- Create artwork from basic shapes.
- Adjust the corners of live shapes.
- Navigate an Illustrator document efficiently.
- Activate Typekit fonts.
- Add type to a document.

Chapter ACA Objectives

For full descriptions of the objectives, see the table on pages 196–204.

DOMAIN 2.0
PROJECT SETUP AND INTERFACE
2.1, 2.2, 2.3, 2.3a, 2.3c, 2.5a, 2.6b

DOMAIN 4.0
CREATE AND MODIFY VISUAL ELEMENTS
4.1a, 4.2a, 4.3b, 4.5a, 4.5c

CHAPTER 2

Creating a Postcard in Illustrator

In this chapter you'll be creating a postcard advertisement for a brand of a reusable water bottle. In the process, you'll be introduced to various concepts that you'll be able to apply to other projects as well as many techniques you'll use every day when working with Adobe Illustrator CC. This chapter is a foundational chapter that builds on basic techniques that can be used to create many types of artwork and projects.

Creating a New Document

Each project will begin with you creating a new document. When creating a new document, you want to keep in mind the intended purpose of the file. What will the file you create be used for? Is it a graphic to be used on the web? Will it be utilized in a video project? Or will it be a print product such as a business card, postcard, or logo to be used in other printed products? The answers to these questions are important at the document creation stage because they will determine which settings you use to create the document.

★ *ACA Objective 2.1*

▶ **Video 2.1** *Create a New Illustrator Document*

To begin creating a new document in Illustrator, do one of the following:

- From the Start workspace in Illustrator, click the Create New button (**Figure 2.1**).
- Choose File > New from the menu bar at the top of the screen (**Figure 2.2**).

Next you will be presented with the New Document dialog box, where you'll see several options to control how the new document will be created (**Figure 2.3**). At the top of the dialog box, you'll see seven categories that determine the general properties that will define your document once it's created.

The categories across the top of the dialog box determine general settings for the document that you create. Here is a description of each category:

- **Recent:** Lists recent document types that you've used before, providing quick access to those settings should you need to use them again.

- **Saved:** Lists any saved templates that you've downloaded within Illustrator.

- **Mobile:** Includes documents at sizes used by common mobile devices such as iPhone, iPad, Apple Watch, Android devices, and Surface Pro. Presets in this category use the RGB color mode, with Raster Effects set to 72 ppi, and use pixels as the default unit of measurement.

- **Web:** Includes documents at common web page sizes for desktop computer screens. These presets use the RGB color mode, with Raster Effects set to 72 ppi, and use pixels as the default unit of measurement.

- **Print:** Includes common print paper sizes such as letter, legal, and tabloid. These presets use the CMYK color mode, with Raster Effects set to 300 ppi, and use points as the default unit of measurement.

- **Film & Video:** Includes document sizes for common video standards like HDV, HDTV, and 4K UHD. These presets use the RGB color mode, with Raster Effects set to 72 ppi, and use pixels as the default unit of measurement.

- **Art & Illustration:** Includes presets for common sizes of artwork in both print and web dimensions. Documents created from this category use the RGB color mode, with Raster Effects set to 72 ppi, and use points as the default unit of measurement.

These categories are designed to give you a general starting point, but it's important to know that all of the settings used in each of these presets can be overridden and customized as you see fit.

A postcard is a print-based product, but the New Document dialog box doesn't provide a document preset for it. We'll set up a document from scratch and customize the settings to suit this project (**Figure 2.4**).

1 Start by selecting the Print category at the top of the New Document dialog box.

2 Give the postcard a name by entering it at the top of the Preset Details section to the right of the New Document dialog box.

3   In the Preset Details section, change the units to inches and enter **7** in the Width field and **5 in** in the Height field. The Orientation setting should automatically change to Landscape after you leave the Height field, but if it doesn't, go ahead and select Landscape. Click the Create button.

Figure 2.4 Defining the settings for the new postcard document

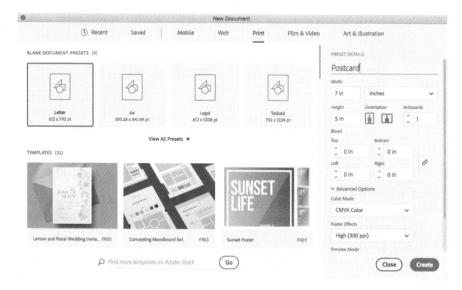

A new document is created with the name that you provided and using the parameters defined in the New Document dialog box. This postcard doesn't need to print right up to the edges, so there was no need to add a bleed value for this document.

Choose File > Save and save your document to your hard drive. Because you provided a name when defining the new document, that is the default name used when saving the file. Although Illustrator provides several file formats in which you can save the document, the Adobe Illustrator format (`.ai`) is the native format used by Illustrator and is very versatile when working with other Adobe products.

★ *ACA Objective 2.2*

Defining Preferences in Adobe Illustrator CC

 **Video 2.2**
*Defining
Preferences
in Adobe
Illustrator CC*

Everyone uses Illustrator in a different way. Illustrators draw various types of artwork, designers create logos, other artists create technical drawings...the list goes on and on. The point is that not everyone uses Illustrator in the same way, and therefore each person has her own style of working and her own preferences for how she likes the program to behave.

Fortunately, it's easy to set up Illustrator the way you want it. Let's take a look at some of the settings that we can adjust for our postcard document.

1 Choose Illustrator CC > Preferences > General (macOS) or Edit > Preferences > General (Windows) to open the Preferences dialog box. Although this takes us directly to the General Preferences, you'll notice a number of other preference categories as well.

2 Click Units to choose your preferred unit of measurement (**Figure 2.5**). Because you chose inches when creating the document, that is the unit that is currently chosen from the General menu. Note that you can choose the units used for Stroke and Type independently.

Figure 2.5 Illustrator allows you to choose your preferred units of measurement.

3 Click User Interface to change the appearance of the program. Illustrator uses the Medium Dark Brightness setting by default. This setting controls the darkness of the main interface elements. Some users like this setting, and others don't. That's why it's a preference! Select the Brightness setting that makes sense for you.

4 Click Performance to set parameters that affect how Illustrator uses your computer's hardware to work more efficiently.

Illustrator uses the GPU (graphics processing unit) on the graphics card in your computer to draw data to the screen faster if Illustrator supports it. You'll know because the GPU Performance section of the dialog box will say "Compatible GPU available." The GPU Performance check box will be selected, and the GPU Details section will list the specifications of your graphics card. If GPU Performance is dimmed, that indicates that your computer doesn't have a compatible GPU available, and therefore Illustrator can't use graphics acceleration.

Illustrator allows you to disable the graphics card (which can be useful for troubleshooting) by deselecting GPU Performance. You can also deselect Animated Zoom if you prefer to zoom using the Marquee method in Illustrator.

5   Click OK to close the Preferences dialog box.

Adding Guides to the Postcard for Easy Alignment of Objects

★ *ACA Objective 2.3*

 **Video 2.3** *Adding Guides to a Document*

Guides are helpful when you need a perfectly straight vertical or horizontal line to serve as a reference for design elements. In this section, you'll add some guides to the Illustrator document to do just that.

Adding Guides

For our postcard, we need a nice, even border around all the sides of the card as well as a gutter in the middle of the card to divide objects horizontally. If your project contains objects that need to be aligned just so, or that should be a specific distance from other objects, the Guides feature in Illustrator is your friend.

It's important to understand that guides are nonprinting elements. They're used during the design and creation phase, but they'll never show up in the final product. If you want to display or hide the guides in a document, choose View > Guides > Show Guides or View > Guides > Hide Guides. You'll often want to hide or show guides on the fly while you're working; you can press Command+; (macOS) or Ctrl+; (Windows) or click the Show/Hide Guides button ⊞ in the Properties panel.

1   Start by switching to the Essentials Classic workspace by choosing Window > Workspace > Essentials Classic. Then choose Window > Workspace > Reset Essentials Classic to ensure that the panels you'll be using in this chapter are available.

2   In order to add guides to a document, you need to display the rulers. Choose View > Rulers > Show Rulers or click the Show/Hide Rulers icon ⌐ in the Properties panel. You'll see rulers displayed along the left side and top of the Document window.

Figure 2.6 Changing the unit of measurement for the document by right-clicking the ruler

Rulers are doubly beneficial. Not only do they allow you to create guides, but they also let you change the unit of measurement for a document. Right-click the left or top ruler to open a menu listing the units available (**Figure 2.6**). Choose the unit that you wish to use, and it becomes the default unit of measurement for the document.

3 Drag from the top ruler down into the document to create a guide. Position the guide so that it is about .25 inches away from the top edge of the document. Watch the left ruler as you drag, and you'll see your location in the document (look for the 1/4-inch mark). Drag out a second guide, but position it about .25 inches away from the bottom edge of the document (**Figure 2.7**).

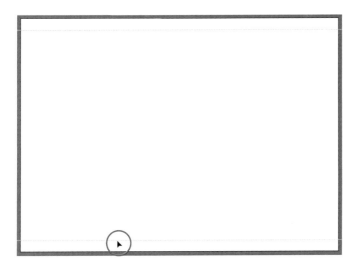

Figure 2.7 Dragging guides from the top ruler to add them to the document

Guides in Illustrator are like any other object; they can be selected by clicking. If you're struggling to position your guides exactly where you want them, open the Transform panel by choosing Window > Transform. Using the Selection tool, select the top guide, then enter **.25** in the Y field, and press Return/Enter. Repeat for the bottom guide but enter **4.75** in the Y field.

4 Drag out guides from the ruler along the left side of the Document window to .25 inches away from the left edge of the document and .25 inches away from the right edge.

5 Drag another vertical guide onto the document from the left ruler and position it at 3.5 inches, which is exactly the horizontal center of the page.

6 Choose Window > Transform to open the Transform panel.

7 Select the guide at the center of the document. In the Transform panel, enter **–.0625** in the X field to the right of the current value and press Return/Enter. Illustrator does the calculation for you and moves the guide 1/16" to the left of its current position (**Figure 2.8**).

Figure 2.8 Adjusting the position of a guide using the Transform panel

8 With the guide still selected, enter **+.125** to the right of the current value of the X field in the Transform panel. Hold down Option (macOS) or Alt (Windows) and press Return/Enter. Illustrator calculates the measurement and creates a copy of the guide at the calculated value. You have now created an 1/8" gutter in the center of the postcard. Repeat these steps to create a horizontal gutter in the middle of the postcard.

★ ACA Objective 4.5c

★ ACA Objective 2.5a

Creating Shapes for the Postcard Background

▶ **Video 2.4**
Creating Shapes for the Background of the Postcard Project

Illustrator gives us the ability to draw virtually any shape that we wish, including squares, rectangles, ovals, circles, polygons, and stars. These are all created using different shape tools, and you can see them by clicking and holding on the currently selected shape tool (Rectangle is the default) (**Figure 2.9**).

1 Start by selecting the Rectangle tool. Then drag from the intersection of the guides in the upper-left corner of the postcard to the intersection of the guides in the middle of the postcard (**Figure 2.10**).

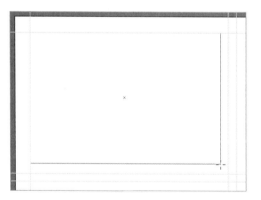

Figure 2.10 Drawing a rectangle in the upper-left quadrant of the postcard

Figure 2.9 The various shape tools available in Illustrator

Depending on the last setting you used in Illustrator, the shape that you've drawn may have a fill or stroke applied or it may have no fill or stroke. You'll change that next.

2 At the bottom of the Tools panel, you'll see the Fill indicator ◨ and the Stroke indicator ◪. The **fill** of an object is the color that an object is filled with, whereas the **stroke** is the border or frame of the object. With the shape selected, click the Fill indicator and open the Swatches panel by choosing

Window > Swatches or by clicking the Swatches panel icon. Click an orange color to apply that color to the selected shape.

3   We need to create a few more shapes for the postcard, but to save time, we'll reuse the shape we've just drawn and make a copy of it. Using the Selection tool, hold down Option (macOS) or Alt (Windows) and drag the rectangle down to the lower-left quadrant of the postcard. Let go of the mouse button and you'll have a duplicate of the original rectangle.

4   Using the Swatches panel, change the color of the second rectangle to yellow.

Drawing a Shape Using the Shaper Tool

★ ACA Objective 4.5a

There's more than one way to skin a cat in Illustrator. In addition to the powerful shape tools, you can use the Shaper tool 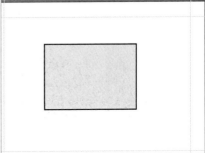 to draw the shape that you want by hand and Illustrator will generate a perfect shape for you.

1   Select the Shaper tool. On the right side of the postcard, use your mouse to draw a rectangle. It doesn't have to be perfect; just a rough approximation (which is about all you can do with a mouse) is all you need to achieve the desired result. When you let go of the mouse, the rectangle will be created with a default fill and stroke (**Figure 2.11**).

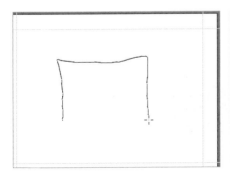
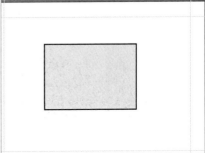

Figure 2.11 Drawing a rectangle using the Shaper tool (left); the result (right)

2   Using the Fill and Stroke indicators at the bottom of the Tools panel, change the fill to a green color and the stroke to None. None refers to removing a stroke or fill from an object and is represented by a red slash in the Swatches panel, Control panel, and Properties panel to represent no color applied.

3   Using the Selection tool, resize the rectangle to fill the two quadrants on the right side of the postcard. Note that when you resize an object, by default the object will snap to the guides, making it easy to resize the shape to the correct size.

Changing the Corner Radius of Shapes in Illustrator

▶ Video 2.5
Changing the Corner Appearance of an Object for the Postcard

When you draw shapes in Illustrator using the Rectangle, Ellipse, Polygon, or Shaper tools, they are created as Live Shapes. Live Shapes are shapes that can be dynamically adjusted after creation. In the case of an ellipse, you can change the start and end point, creating a sort of Pac-Man shape or a pie wedge. In the case of a polygon, you can change the number of sides in the polygon dynamically. In the case of a rectangle, you can dynamically adjust the corners of the shape after creation, making it easy to round corners on the object. These adjustable corners are called "Live Corners."

1   Select the orange rectangle with the Selection tool. You'll notice that a Live Corners widget ◉ appears in each corner of the rectangle. Drag any of the widgets away from the corner, and notice that all of the corners of the shape become rounded. Option-click (macOS) or Alt-click (Windows) a widget to change the type of corner applied to the shape. Drag the widget back to the corner to remove the adjustment.

2   In this example, we want to affect only some of the corners of the shape, not all of them. Using the Direct Selection tool, click the anchor point of the top-left corner of the shape. Now drag the widget away from the corner and notice that only that corner is changing.

3   To achieve more accuracy, you can use the Transform panel, which you open by choosing Window > Transform. Make sure the shape properties are being displayed by clicking the panel menu icon and choosing Show Options (if the menu includes Hide Options, that means all of the options are already being displayed). In the bottom half of the panel you'll see settings for the corner type and radius for each of the four corners of the shape. Deselect Link Corner Radius Values to prevent all corners from changing at the same time.

4   In the Transform panel, click the Corner Type icon for the upper-left corner and choose Round from the options; then change its Corner Radius value to **.25 in** (**Figure 2.12**).

5   Repeat steps 3 and 4 and change the lower-left corner of the yellow shape and then change both corners on the right side of the green shape (**Figure 2.13**).

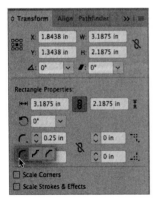

Figure 2.12 Changing the corner type and radius of the selected shape

Figure 2.13 The result of rounding the corners of the shapes on the postcard

Navigating a Document Effectively in Illustrator

★ *ACA Objective 2.3a*

One of the most important things you can learn when working in Illustrator is the ability to efficiently navigate a document. Being able to get around and focus on specific objects is key to being able to work efficiently and in a timely manner. Knowing how to use Illustrator without being able to navigate a document effectively is like memorizing a map of where you live but not knowing how to ride a bike or drive a car. It becomes a limitation. So let's walk through how to navigate a document in Illustrator.

▶ **Video 2.6**
Navigating an Illustrator Document Using Various Techniques

The first thing you'll learn is how to zoom in on an element in the document to see it more closely. I often watch users work, and they squint to see a certain area of their document. Zooming doesn't cost any money! Use the Zoom tool!

1 Select the Zoom tool ⌕ in the Tools panel.

2 To use the Zoom tool, do one of the following:

- If Animated Zoom is enabled, place the mouse cursor over the center of the object that you want to zoom in on and drag to the right to zoom in on the object (**Figure 2.14**). Zoom in as much as you want. To zoom out, drag to the left.

Figure 2.14 Zooming in on an area of the postcard

- If Animated Zoom is disabled, drag a marquee around the object that you want to zoom in on. To zoom out, hold down Option (macOS) or Alt (Windows) and click to zoom out incrementally or drag to create a small marquee area to zoom out.

3 Zoom back in to another area of the document. Often, once you've zoomed in on an area, you realize that you want to look at a different area of the document. Although you could use the scroll bars on the right and bottom of the Document window, you can pan more efficiently using the Hand tool. Select the Hand tool ✋ and drag in your document to a new area.

4 To quickly get back to a view of the entire document, you can use a popular keyboard shortcut. Press Command+0 (macOS) or Ctrl+0 (Windows) to force your document to fit to the current Illustrator window.

I think you'll agree that these tools are powerful. Believe it or not, you can perform these functions without ever selecting the tools in the Tools panel. Instead, you can use some keyboard combinations to achieve the desired result. The benefit of using this technique is that once you've zoomed or panned to the desired location, simply let go of the keyboard combination and you're right where you left off, with the current tool selected. This allows you to spend more time working and less time selecting tools in Illustrator.

1 Hold Command+spacebar (macOS) or Ctrl+spacebar (Windows) to activate the Zoom tool. Keeping the keys held down, drag in the document to zoom in to the desired area. When you're done, let go of the keys and you're back to whichever tool was active before zooming in on the document.

2 Now once you're zoomed in, simply hold down the spacebar on your keyboard to activate the Hand tool temporarily. Drag to pan to a different area of the document. When you're done, release the spacebar to return to the default tool that was active before you started panning. Pretty cool!

NOTE

When using the Command+spacebar shortcut in macOS, you may notice that Spotlight appears on your screen. If it does, you can simply ignore it and zoom in on the desired element. If this bothers you, you can change the keyboard shortcut for Spotlight by choosing System Preferences from the Apple menu and then clicking Keyboard. In the Keyboard preferences pane, click Shortcuts and select Spotlight from the list on the left side of the dialog box. Deselect Show Spotlight Search to prevent Spotlight from opening when you use Command+spacebar to zoom.

Adding Text to the Postcard

★ *ACA Objective 4.2a*

▶ *Video 2.7 Using the Type Tool to Add Text Elements to the Postcard*

Most projects you create in Illustrator will require text to convey the message that you're trying to get across. Illustrator contains powerful functionality for creating and styling text. For this postcard, we will add a few paragraphs to convey the message and to achieve (we hope) the marketing objective for the project.

Activating Typekit Fonts

One of the challenges when designing a project is choosing an appropriate font for the design that you're creating. Choosing the font isn't often the biggest problem you'll face, but figuring out if you own the font or if the font is active on your system might be. I can't tell you that every font you'll ever need is easily available to you, but I can tell you that a ton of them are! As a Creative Cloud subscriber, you have access to the Portfolio version of the Typekit library, which contains more than 5,700 fonts of varying styles for you to choose from. To use Typekit, you simply need an Internet connection. Log into Typekit using your Adobe ID and password.

1   Choose Type > Add Fonts From Typekit. This will display the Typekit web page in your default browser. If you're not already signed in, you'll be asked to provide your Adobe ID and password.

2   For this project, you can choose any font that you wish. Feel free to browse the Typekit site and explore the various fonts that are available to you for activation. We want something fun yet bold for the postcard, and if you'd like to follow along with what was shown in the video, type **abril** in the search field at the top of the Typekit web page. Choose Abril from the list of results, and you'll be shown all of the faces available within that font. If you know which faces you'd like to use, click the Sync button to the right of each face that you want to use, but if you want to make all of the faces available, click the Sync All button at the top of the page.

An alert will appear when your fonts have been synced, and (depending on your notification Preference settings) a notification pop-up window may open to let you know that the fonts have been synced to your computer.

Adding and Formatting Text

Illustrator creates two different types of type object: point type and area type. Point type is created by simply clicking anywhere in the document with the Type tool. Illustrator will automatically insert the text *Lorem ipsum*, but you can change that to whatever you wish. Point type doesn't flow within a given area but instead will continue in one long, continuous line of text until you manually insert a line break (by pressing Return/Enter), after which you can continue typing. If you switch to the Selection tool and drag a handle on the bounding box that surrounds the type object to change the shape of the box, the text will change shape to match. You can scale point type proportionally by holding Shift as you drag one of the handles. Point type is typically best used for a more artistic type of work.

The second type of type object that Illustrator creates is called an area type object. Area type objects are created by dragging with the Type tool to define a shape. Text that you type into this shape flows to fill the shape. Illustrator inserts *Lorem ipsum* into this object as well (**Figure 2.15**), but after you replace it with your own text, you'll notice that the text automatically wraps within the area type object that you've drawn. If you switch to the Selection tool and drag a handle of the object, you'll see the type within the area type object just rewraps within the container and conforms to the size of the area type object. Area type is best used when your text needs to fit within a given area and must be structured in paragraphs. For the postcard, you'll create both point type and area type objects.

Figure 2.15 Creating a point type object on the postcard

1 Return to Illustrator and select the Type tool. Click in the orange rectangle in the upper-left corner of the artboard to create a point type object. Type the text **When Life Gives You Lemons…**.

2 Using the Type tool, drag across the yellow rectangle to create an area type object slightly smaller than the yellow rectangle. Type the text **Slice them, and put them in your reusable water bottle!**.

3 Select the text that you created in the previous step, and in the Properties panel, open the top menu in the Character section (the Font Family menu). Click the TK button at the top of the menu to filter out non-Typekit fonts, and then choose Abril Fatface Regular from the list of fonts (**Figure 2.16**).

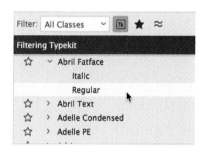

Figure 2.16 Choosing a font from the Font Family menu in the Properties panel

4 With the text still selected, use the Font Size controls on the Properties panel to change the size to 15 pt.

5 The text will look better if it's displayed on two lines, so if necessary, use the Selection tool to adjust the size of the area type object by dragging the handles until the text flows onto two lines.

6 Go back to the first type object that you created, which is currently a point type object. The text will be easier to work with if this is an area type object, so select the text with the Selection tool and double-click the circle that protrudes from the right side of the object (**Figure 2.17**). The point type object is converted to an area type object.

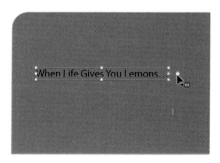

Figure 2.17 Converting a point type object to an area type object

7 Select the text using the Type tool. Change the font to Abril Fatface Regular and set the point size to 21 pt.

8 Switch to the Selection tool and change the size of the area type object so that the word *Lemons* wraps to the second line.

9 Select the word *Lemons* with the Type tool and change the font style to italic, the size to 44 pt, and the leading to 37 pt. Adjust the type object using the Selection tool so that the text fits within the box. Change the text color to white.

10 Create one last area type object and type the text **Bring this postcard to your local retailer for 20% off a new water bottle.** Set the font to Myriad Pro Regular, the size to 9 pt, and the leading to 11 pt. Position this toward the bottom of the yellow rectangle.

Adjust the objects on the postcard as you see fit and to make things appear the way that you want them.

★ *ACA Objective 4.1a*

★ *ACA Objective 4.3b*

★ *ACA Objective 2.6b*

▶ **Video 2.8** *Drawing a Lemon Using Basic Shape Tools in Adobe Illustrator CC*

Drawing the Basic Lemon Artwork

To finish up our postcard, we need some compelling artwork on the right side of the postcard. We could find lemon artwork from a variety of sources, but we can fairly easily create a clean, modern-looking lemon by using some basic shapes in Illustrator.

1 Make sure nothing in the artwork is selected; then select the Fill color box in the Properties panel. Open the Swatches panel and select a nice, lemony yellow swatch.

2 Select the Ellipse tool ⬭, and then Shift-drag on top of the green rectangle on the right side of the postcard to draw a perfect circle.

3 Switch to the Direct Selection tool ▷. and click the bottom anchor point of the circle to select it.

4 Drag down on the anchor point to elongate the circle, turning it into somewhat of an egg shape (a lemon shape, really) (**Figure 2.18**). While the Selection tool selects objects or **groups** as a unit, the Direct Selection tool modifies the fundamental elements of an object, giving you control over the shape of the object that you're working with.

5 Switch back to the Selection tool and adjust the width and height of the shape until you're happy with it.

6 Select the Ellipse tool again and draw a horizontal oval at the top of the lemon shape, slightly protruding from the top of the lemon (**Figure 2.19**).

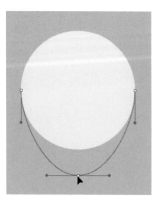

Figure 2.18 Dragging an anchor point with the Direct Selection tool

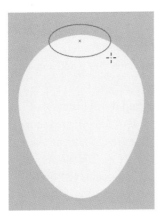

Figure 2.19 Drawing an oval-shaped ellipse on the top of the first shape

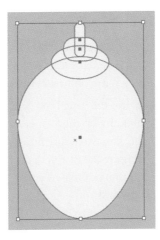

Figure 2.20 The shapes that are making up the top portion of the lemon

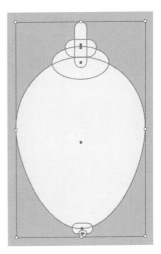

Figure 2.21 The shapes that make up the overall lemon shape

7   Select the Rounded Rectangle tool ▢. Draw a horizontal rounded rectangle above the oval that you drew previously, making it slightly narrower than the oval and protruding from the top of the oval.

8   Using the Rectangle tool, draw a vertical rectangle that protrudes from the top of the lemon shapes and extends a bit from the top. Use **Figure 2.20** as a reference.

9   Switch back to the Selection tool, and click the rectangle. You'll see a Live Corner widget in each corner of the shape. Drag one of the widgets toward the center of the rectangle to round the corners of the rectangle. Adjust until you like the way that it looks (Figure 2.20).

10   Using the Rounded Rectangle tool, draw a small rounded rectangle at the bottom of the lemon, partially overlapping the edge of the larger shape.

11   Switch to the Ellipse tool and draw a small, horizontal oval overlapping the bottom edge of the rounded rectangle that you drew in the previous step (**Figure 2.21**).

Use your artistic judgment to draw this lemon. Yours doesn't need to look like the one that's drawn in the figures. Be creative! But if you want some guidance, use the figures in this section of the book as a reference.

> **NOTE**
>
> *If after drawing the vertical rectangle at the top of the lemon shape you don't see the widgets, you may need to zoom in further on the selected art to see them.*

Embellishing the Lemon

Now that you've drawn the main shape of the lemon, let's add some details to give it a bit of realism. First, you'll sketch a leaf to its stem end; then you'll add some reflections to give the fruit a sense of three-dimensionality.

Figure 2.22 Drawing a squiggly line with the Pencil tool to represent the leaf at the top of the lemon

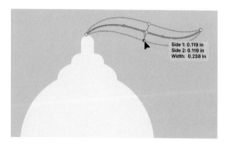

Figure 2.23 Using the Width tool to vary the weight of a stroke at a specific point along a path

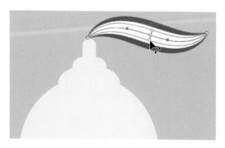

Figure 2.24 Using the Width tool to vary the weight of the accent stroke that is on top of the green leaf path

1 Select the Pencil tool ![pencil icon] (you'll find it by clicking and holding on the Shaper tool), and draw an S-shaped squiggly line extending horizontally from the top of the lemon (**Figure 2.22**). You're drawing a single leaf for the lemon, so think of that as you're drawing the line. If you draw the line and you're not happy with it, simply choose Edit > Undo and try it again.

2 Open the Swatches panel, select Stroke, and select a dark green color.

3 Select the Width tool ![width tool icon]. Starting at the midpoint of the squiggly line, drag away from the line at a right angle to it. The Width tool varies the weight of the stroke of a path (or a variable-width stroke) at the point where you drag. You can use the Width tool to create amazing organic shapes very easily. Drag until you're happy with the shape and it represents a leaf atop the lemon (**Figure 2.23**).

4 With the Selection tool, select the leaf shape that you just drew. Choose Edit > Copy, and then choose Edit > Paste In Front. This puts a copy of the leaf directly on top of the original one.

5 With the pasted leaf (path) still selected, change the stroke color to white. Using the Width tool, adjust the width point that you added previously and reduce the stroke width of the white stroke, creating a highlight on the leaf of the lemon (**Figure 2.24**).

6 Use what you've learned to add another white highlight by drawing a path along the right side of the lemon and varying the width using the Width tool.

You're almost finished! The one last finishing touch we're going to add to our postcard is the addition of a few triangles that point to the key information of the postcard.

7 Select the Shaper tool . Using your mouse, draw a rough representation of a triangle and then let go of the mouse (**Figure 2.25**). You don't have to be very precise when you use this tool. You should notice that upon releasing the mouse button, Illustrator creates a perfect triangle for you to use.

8 Set the stroke of the triangle to None and the fill to white.

9 Using the Selection tool, rotate the triangle by hovering over the corners of its bounding box and dragging the triangle to the desired angle. You can hold down Shift as you rotate to snap the rotation angle to 45-degree increments. You can scale the triangle proportionally by Shift-dragging a handle.

Figure 2.25 Drawing a triangle using the Shaper tool

10 Size and position the triangle to replicate the finished postcard in **Figure 2.26**. Make a copy of the triangle for the second instance of the triangle.

Figure 2.26 The finished postcard with the triangle shapes in position

Way to go! You finished your first project using Adobe Illustrator! You may not realize it at this point, but you've been exposed to a lot of foundational features of Illustrator. Every project you create from here on will use the skills that you learned in this chapter as a foundation on which you can build and learn.

CHAPTER OBJECTIVES

Chapter Learning Objectives

- Edit and modify artboards.
- Use the Shape Builder tool.
- Add and format text.
- Create and modify swatches.
- Convert text to outlines.
- Use the Color Guide panel to create swatches.
- Use the Pathfinder panel to modify objects.

Chapter ACA Objectives

For full descriptions of the objectives, see the table on pages 196–204.

DOMAIN 2.0
PROJECT SETUP AND INTERFACE
2.2a, 2.3a, 2.3c, 2.3d, 2.5a, 2.5c, 2.5d

DOMAIN 4.0
CREATE AND MODIFY VISUAL ELEMENTS
4.2a, 4.2b, 4.2c, 4.2d, 4.3c, 4.4a, 4.4b, 4.5b

CHAPTER 3

Creating the Front of a Business Card

In this chapter, you'll be creating the front of a business card for a skate-board shop called Session Skate Shop. Throughout the chapter, you'll be learning techniques that go beyond the basics, and you'll learn how to create artistic elements and achieve visual results in Adobe Illustrator CC using those techniques.

★ ACA Objective 2.2a

★ ACA Objective 2.3a

★ ACA Objective 4.4a

▶ Video 3.1
Modifying Artboards

Modifying an Artboard

When creating a project in Illustrator, you begin with at least one artboard. Think of an artboard as the working area in a document. Illustrator supports multiple artboards in a document, which is useful when you're creating multiple versions of a project or for projects that contain several elements such as a business card with a letterhead and an envelope. Each item could live on its own artboard. Don't think of artboards as pages but instead as artwork holders. Illustrator isn't a page layout program, so the term "pages" doesn't really apply. That would be more appropriate for a true page layout application such as Adobe InDesign.

Often during the design process, you may not always know how big your artboard should be. Sometimes you'll simply start with a working area and then decide what size the artboard should be later on. Illustrator lets you modify the dimensions of an artboard "on the fly" so you can make adjustments to it at any stage.

Start by creating a new document in Adobe Illustrator. Size isn't important right now. In Video 3.1 we used a letter-sized document in case you want to follow along.

With a new document created, you can modify the artboard in a number of ways. You can do any of the following:

- Select the Artboard tool 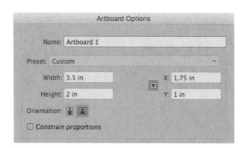, and drag any of the handles on the sides or corners of the artboard.

- With the Artboard tool selected, change the dimensions and/or the X/Y coordinates in the Control panel at the top of the Illustrator interface or in the Properties panel.

- Double-click the icon at the far right of the artboard in the Artboards panel to display the Artboard Options dialog box; change the dimensions and/or coordinates of the artboard, and then click OK (**Figure 3.1**).

Figure 3.1 Changing the artboard dimensions in the Artboard Options dialog box

- Double-click the Artboard tool or click the Artboard Options button in the Control panel or the Properties panel to display the Artboard Options dialog box and change the dimensions and/or coordinates of the artboard; then click OK.

To create a new artboard, click the New Artboard icon in the Control panel or the Properties panel or at the bottom of the Artboards panel (**Figure 3.2**). Selecting an existing artboard in the Artboards panel first will define the dimensions that will be used for the new artboard created.

Figure 3.2 Creating a new artboard by clicking the New Artboard button at the bottom of the Artboards panel

In some cases, you may want to duplicate an artboard. This can be helpful if you want to create a second artboard with the exact same artwork on it but you plan to modify the artwork on the copied artboard.

1 Choose Window > Workspace > Essentials Classic; then choose Window > Workspace > Reset Essentials Classic to make sure all of the tools and panels you need for this lesson will be available.

2 Select the Artboard tool and Option-drag (macOS) or Alt-drag (Windows) the artboard to where you would like the new artboard positioned. This will make a copy of the artboard.

3. To ensure that the artwork on the original artboard is also duplicated, make sure that Move/Copy Artwork With Artboard button  is selected in the Control panel or that Move Artwork With Artboard is checked in the Properties panel.

4. If you prefer to make a copy of only the artboard, simply deselect Move/Copy Artwork With Artboard.

As you add more artboards to a document, the default artboard names are simply Artboard 1, Artboard 2, and so on. It helps to name your artboards so that you can easily identify each one as you're working and to aid in navigating to a specific artboard more easily. To rename an artboard, do one of the following:

- Double-click the name of the artboard in the Artboards panel, type a new name, then press Return (macOS) or Enter (Windows) (**Figure 3.3**).

- Click the icon at the far right of the artboard in the Artboards panel to display the Artboard Options dialog box. Type a new name in the Name field; then click OK.

- Click the Artboard Options button in the Control panel to open the Artboard Options dialog box. Type a new name in the Name field; then click OK.

- Rename the artboard in the Properties panel directly when the Artboard tool is selected.

Figure 3.3 Renaming an artboard in the Artboards panel

For our business card project, we need a background element that will serve as the foundation for the card.

1. Using the Rectangle tool, click anywhere on the artboard to display the Rectangle dialog box. Enter **3.5 in** for the Width and **2 in** for the Height. Click OK.

2. With the new rectangle created, set the stroke to none and the fill to a color of your choice. Position the rectangle anywhere on the artboard.

3. Select the rectangle using the Selection tool, and then switch to the Artboard tool. Choose Fit To Selected Art from the Preset menu in the Control or Properties panel (**Figure 3.4**). This resizes the artboard to make it the exact size of the selected artwork.

Figure 3.4 Changing the size of the artboard to fit the size of the selected artwork

4. Name the Artboard **Front** in the Control panel or the Properties panel.

- Select the Selection tool to switch focus away from the artboard.

- Save the document as **Business Card**.

★ *ACA Objective 2.3c*

★ *ACA Objective 2.3d*

★ *ACA Objective 2.5a*

★ *ACA Objective 2.5c*

★ *ACA Objective 4.5b*

▶ **Video 3.2** *Creating a Half-Pipe for the Business Card*

Creating a Half-Pipe for the Background of the Card

The front of the business card that we're creating has a half-pipe for the background art. If you think about drawing this art from scratch, it might seem daunting, but if you think about some basic shapes that make up the final shape of the half-pipe, it's really not that complex. Thanks to the power of Illustrator, we can create this art quite easily.

Adding Bleed to the Card

Before we go too far, you should realize that the design for the card has the half-pipe shape extending to the edge of the card. Because a printing press (and most desktop printers for that matter) are unable to print ink to the edge of a piece of paper, the artwork needs to be printed on a larger piece of paper, with the art-work extending past the edge of the project. Then after printing, the card can be trimmed down to the final size, creating the desired end result for the project. The distance the printed artwork needs to extend beyond the actual project is called **bleed**. In the next steps, you'll add bleed to the card, defined by guides, and extend the artwork to the bleed guides.

1 Choose File > Document Setup. In the Document Setup dialog box, make sure the Make All Settings The Same button ▯ is selected and enter **.125 in** in one of the Bleed fields. Press the Tab key to exit the field, and all of the bleed values should update to the same value (**Figure 3.5**). Click OK.

Figure 3.5 Entering the bleed value for the card in the Document Setup dialog box

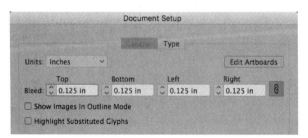

2 Using the Selection tool, extend the sides of the rectangle so they snap to the bleed guides that appear on each side of the artboard. This provides adequate bleed for the artwork.

3 Position two vertical guides on the card that are 1/8 inches away from the left and right sides of the card. If you need to modify the position of the guides

after dragging them to the artboard, choose View > Guides > Unlock Guides to unlock them so that you can adjust the position of the guides.

4   Select the rectangle with the Selection tool and double-click the Fill indicator at the bottom of the Tools panel to display the color picker. Choose a light brown color, or if you'd like to follow along with the video, enter the following values: C: **27**, M: **52**, Y: **84**, K: **8**. Click OK.

Creating the Half-Pipe Using the Shape Builder Tool

Now you'll create the actual shape of the half-pipe using the rectangle that you've already created as a foundation.

1   Draw a new rectangle between the two vertical guides that you created. Extend the bottom of the rectangle about two-thirds down from the top of the business card and extend the top way above the top of the business card, as shown in **Figure 3.6**. (For the sake of visibility, I've given this new rectangle a contrasting fill color.)

2   With the rectangle still selected, drag one of the corner widgets toward the center of the rectangle to round the corners of the shape. Don't drag the corner widget to its limit! For a realistic half-pipe, you'll want a little bit of flat at the bottom middle of the rectangle.

3   Using the Selection tool, select both of the shapes.

4   Switch to the Shape Builder tool 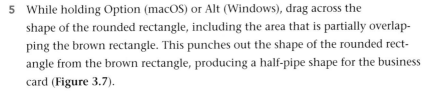 and hover over the artwork. You'll see different portions of the shapes highlight as your cursor passes over them, including areas where the two shapes overlap.

The job of the Shape Builder tool is to create new shapes from existing shapes. Using the Shape Builder tool, if you drag across several areas, the tool will merge those areas together into one. Conversely, if you Option+click (macOS) or Alt+click (Windows) an element, it will be deleted.

5   While holding Option (macOS) or Alt (Windows), drag across the shape of the rounded rectangle, including the area that is partially overlapping the brown rectangle. This punches out the shape of the rounded rectangle from the brown rectangle, producing a half-pipe shape for the business card (**Figure 3.7**).

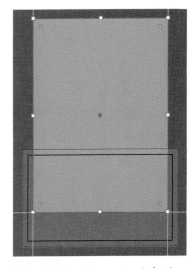

Figure 3.6 Drawing a rectangle for the half-pipe artwork

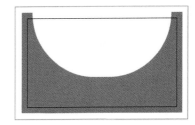

Figure 3.7 Punching out the rounded rectangle shape from the brown rectangle shape, producing the half-pipe shape

★ ACA Objective 4.2a

★ ACA Objective 4.2b

★ ACA Objective 4.2c

▶ **Video 3.3** *Adding Text for the Logotype of the Business Card*

Adding Text for the Logotype

Every business needs a brand. For the Session Skate Shop, we'll create a logotype element that the business can use as a unique mark that is easily identifiable and attractive to clients. Illustrator has powerful text tools that we'll take advantage of in this section, and you'll learn a lot of the options that are available when you're working with text.

At this point in the project, we no longer need the guides that we created earlier. We may need them later, so we don't want to delete them, but we're done with them for now. So if you'd like, you can hide the guides by choosing View > Guides > Hide Guides.

Adding the Text

The logotype we'll create is more than one line, so we'll create an area type object to contain the text for the logotype.

1 Using the Type tool, drag to create an area type object that is roughly half the width of the card but centered at the top within the open area of the half-pipe.

2 Lorem ipsum text appears in the area type object. Type the word **Session**; then press Return/Enter and type **Sk8shop**.

3 Change the font of the text to Fresno Black. Keep in mind that this is a Typekit font, so if you don't see it available on your computer, you may have to activate the font or simply use a different font of your choosing.

4 In the Character panel, change the size of the word *Session* to 48 pt and the size of the word *Sk8shop* to 32 pt. In the event that the text becomes overset and doesn't fit within the area type object, switch to the Selection tool and drag one of the object's handles to enlarge it to accommodate the text.

5 Select the word *Sk8shop* and adjust the leading value to decrease the space between the lines of text until the text is visually appealing.

Adjusting Kerning and Tracking

Kerning and tracking, although similar, are actually two different adjustments. Kerning is the adjustment of the space between two adjacent characters. To kern a pair of characters, select the Text tool and click between the characters you want to adjust to place the insertion point, and then adjust the kerning value. Typically as text increases in size, the space between the characters gets disproportionately larger than what is visually pleasing. In cases like this, kerning is used to adjust the text.

Tracking, in comparison, is the adjustment of the space between characters over a range of text. To track a range of text, select the text using the Type tool and then adjust the tracking value. For the logotype being created, we'll apply both types of adjustments.

1   Using the Type tool, click between the first *S* and *e* in the word *Session*. In the Character panel, click the up and down arrows in the kerning adjustment field to increase or decrease the space between the pair of characters. You can also use the keyboard shortcut Option+left/Right Arrow key (macOS) or Alt+left/Right Arrow key (Windows).

> **NOTE**
>
> *When using the keyboard shortcuts to adjust kerning and tracking, keep in mind that the keyboard increment defined in the Type section in Illustrator Preferences controls the amount of kerning applied with each tap of the arrow key. To adjust the increment used, choose Preferences > Type and change the values. **Figure 3.8** shows the values that I defined for type adjustment when using keyboard shortcuts.*

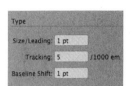

Figure 3.8 Adjusting the increments used when adjusting type using a keyboard shortcut

2   Click between the *e* and the *s* or simply press the Right Arrow key on your keyboard to jump to the next pair of characters and adjust the kerning to the desired amount.

It's important to understand that there's no magic number here. The adjustment of kerning is a visual and often subjective decision. The goal here is to adjust the kerning between characters to make them visually appealing and so that there's no odd spacing between characters. You want the characters to look like they belong together.

3   Using the Type tool, select the word *Sk8shop* and adjust the tracking in the Character panel by clicking the up or down buttons next to the tracking field to increase the space between the characters in the selection (**Figure 3.9**).

Again, this adjustment is for aesthetic reasons, and there's no perfect number. We want the *Sk8shop* text to be approximately the same width

Figure 3.9 Adjusting the tracking to increase the space between the characters of the selected text

as the *Session* text above it. To do this, we could either enlarge the text or increase the tracking, as we're doing here.

4   Using the Type tool, select all of the text in the area type object and click the Align Center button in the Control, Paragraph, or Properties panel.

5   Using the Selection tool, tidy up the area type object to make it as small as possible but still contain the text. Doing this helps to keep the document clean and makes it easier to work with objects in the document.

★ ACA Objective 2.5a

★ ACA Objective 2.5c

★ ACA Objective 2.5d

▶ *Video 3.4*
Creating Swatches for the Front of the Business Card

Creating Swatches

Although it's possible to create colors in Illustrator "on the fly," you have much more control over the colors in a project when you create **swatches**. Swatches give you the ability to consistently apply the same color to different objects, and when swatches are defined as global swatches, you gain the added control of having objects update when you change the color of the original swatch. Now make no mistake, there are certain types of projects that you might create in Illustrator that are of a more artistic nature where you'll need many varying subtle shades of color—and that's okay. For this project, however, we'll be creating swatches and we'll even use the help of Illustrator to pick complementary colors for the initial swatch that we create.

Our client has a brand color that they've decided on, so we'll start by creating a swatch for that color. After that, we need some other colors that complement the brand color. Illustrator is going to help us pick colors that work well with the initial swatch.

1   Open the Swatches panel. Click the panel menu in the upper-right corner of the panel and choose New Swatch (**Figure 3.10**).

Figure 3.10 Creating a new swatch from the Swatches panel menu

2 In the New Swatch dialog box, you should see the initial values of the last color that you used. Change the color mode to CMYK and then enter the following values into the appropriate fields: C: **75**, M: **82**, Y: **15**, B: **3**.

3 Enter **Violet** in the Swatch Name field, select Global, deselect Add To My Library, and click OK.

Selecting Global tells Illustrator that whenever you apply this swatch to an object, it should maintain the connection of that object's color to the swatch. So if you ever decide to change the color values of the swatch, all of the objects in your project that have that color applied will update automatically to match.

> **NOTE**
>
> *At this point, it's a good idea to remove any unused swatches by clicking the panel menu in the Swatches panel and choosing Select Unused Colors. Click the trash can at the bottom of the Swatches panel to delete those swatches that are not being used.*

4 Open the Color Guide panel by choosing Window > Color Guide. The Violet swatch that you just created should be the current color, but if it's not, click the Violet swatch again in the Swatches panel and return to the Color Guide panel.

5 Open the Harmony Rules menu (to the far right of the Base Color swatch) to see the available choices. Harmony rules define relationships between colors that look good together. Choose a harmony rule that you like, or if you'd like to follow along with the video, choose Left Complement.

6 Click the Save Color Group To Swatch Panel button at the bottom of the Color Guide panel. This adds all of the swatches from that harmony rule to the Swatches panel (**Figure 3.11**).

Note that in the Swatches panel, all of the colors that have been added except the initial Violet swatch that you created are not global swatches (there's no triangle in the lower-right corner of the swatch icon). You'll fix that in the next step.

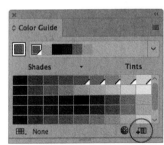

Figure 3.11 Adding the swatches from the harmony rule to the Swatches panel

7 Click the first nonglobal swatch in the group that you just added to the Swatches panel, and then Shift-click the last one to select all of the nonglobal swatches. From the Swatches panel menu in the upper-right corner of the panel, choose Swatch Options. In the Swatch Options dialog box, select Global and click OK. All of the swatches in the group that you just added should now contain a triangle in the lower-right corner.

★ ACA Objective 4.2d

★ ACA Objective 4.3c

▶ **Video 3.5**
*Converting the
Logotype Text
to Paths*

Customizing the Logotype

We want to customize the logotype that we've created to make it look unique—
something that stands out. During the initial design phase, it was determined that
it might look interesting if the first *S* in the word *Session* weaved through the other
letters of the word. This can't be done with live text, so we'll convert the text to
outlines and modify the resulting paths to create the look that we want.

1 Using the Selection tool, select the area type object and apply the Violet color
to the fill of the text.

2 Choose Type > Create Outlines. This converts the text to paths, and the text is
no longer editable.

3 Zoom in on the first *S* of the word *Session* and, using the Direct Selection tool,
click the anchor point at the upper right of the letter *S*. Shift-click the anchor
point below the first anchor point (**Figure 3.12**).

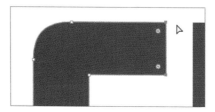

Figure 3.12 Selecting the
two anchor points using the
Direct Selection tool

4 Drag the selected anchor points to the right to extend the shape to the right
edge of the letter *N* in *Session*. To keep the anchor points aligned to their original location, hold down the Shift key on your keyboard as you drag.

Interleaving the Shapes in the Logotype

★ ACA Objective 4.5b

▶ **Video 3.6** *Using
Live Paint to
Enhance the
Logotype*

To further customize the logotype, we'll use the Live Paint feature to make certain
portions of the logotype a different color, creating the illusion of the *S* interleaving
between the other elements of the logotype.

1 Select the logotype group using the Selection tool to make it active.

2 Select the Live Paint Bucket tool ▨ . You'll find it by clicking and holding on
the Shape Builder tool.

3 Hover over the logotype group and click once to convert the logotype to a Live Paint group. Notice that now every component of the overlapping shapes becomes an element that you can apply a different color to by clicking. Each enclosed area in a Live Paint group is called a face, and the boundaries between faces are edges.

It would be helpful if there was a darker version of the Violet swatch that we created earlier, but the harmony rule that was chosen doesn't contain one. We'll create a darker version next so that we have a swatch that we can use.

4 Open the Swatches panel and click the New Swatch icon at the bottom of the panel to create a new swatch based on the Violet swatch.

5 Hold down Shift and drag any of the sliders to the right to adjust all of the sliders at the same time. This maintains the hue of the color but increases or decreases the saturation. When you have a darker version of the Violet swatch, rename the swatch to **Violet Dark**, and then click OK.

6 With the Live Paint Bucket tool still active, click every letter of the word *Session* except the first *S* and then click the top portions of some of the letters to create the appearance of the first *S* shape interleaving between the characters (**Figure 3.13**).

7 Press the Right Arrow or Left Arrow key on your keyboard until the color above the cursor is a lighter shade of the violet color and then apply the light color to the top portion of the letters in between the darker ones. Give the tiny piece in the top-right corner a fill of None (**Figure 3.14**).

Figure 3.13 Coloring different portions of the Live Paint group using the Live Paint Bucket tool

Figure 3.14 Applying a lighter swatch to the top of the alternating characters

Adding Paragraph Text to the Front of the Business Card

★ ACA Objective 4.2c

▶ **Video 3.7** *Adding Paragraph Text to the Front of the Business Card*

The point of a business card is not only to advertise a business but also to provide a way to contact a specific person or persons at that business. Our business card is taking shape, but there's currently no method by which to contact someone at that business. In this section, we'll add the contact information in a paragraph type object.

1 Choose View > Show Guides. Using the Type tool, drag in the lower-left corner of the business card from the intersection of the guides up and to the right to create an area type object. By default the area type object is filled with lorem ipsum text, but the text is selected by default.

2 Type a name, a position, and an email address. You can make it up if you wish, or you can follow along with the example used in the video. Make sure you separate each line with a carriage return by pressing Return/Enter.

3 Change the font to Proxima Soft Light or another font of your choosing, and set the size to 10 pt and the leading to 11 pt. Set the alignment of the text to Align Left.

4 Change the color of the text to the Dark Violet swatch that you created and set the contact name to bold or semibold.

5 Open the Paragraph panel to change the paragraph settings. Select the contact name and increase the Space After Paragraph value to add a bit of space (paragraph spacing) to make the name stand out.

6 Using the Selection tool, Option-drag (macOS) or Alt-drag (Windows) the area type object to the right side of the business card. Replace the first contact's name, title, and email address with the info for a second contact and change the text alignment of all lines to align right (**Figure 3.15**).

Figure 3.15 The business card after adding the contact information to the left and right sides of the card

Finishing Up the Business Card Front ★ ACA Objective 4.4b

The front of the business card is looking good at this point. But as any designer will tell you, there's always more that you can do to the design. In the case of our business card, we can't help but feel as if the half-pipe element might get lost on the customer. So maybe adding an element to make it more obvious would help. In this case, we'll draw a skateboard and position it on the half-pipe to make the element more obvious yet subtle enough that it's not in your face.

▶ **Video 3.8** *Finishing Up the Front of the Card*

Drawing the Skateboard

This exercise introduces the Pen tool, one of Illustrator's signature features. It's famous for being difficult to master, but it's great for drawing straight lines.

1 Select the Pen tool ✐, and, somewhere off to the side of the business card in the white space, click once with the Pen tool to create an anchor point.

2 Hold down the Shift key and click to the right of the first anchor point to create another anchor point. A **line** segment is drawn between the two anchor points.

3 Move the mouse up and to the right a bit, and click once again to create one last anchor point (three anchor points total) and a second line segment (**Figure 3.16**). In case you haven't discovered this yet, you're creating the profile of a skateboard. Press the Escape key on your keyboard to terminate drawing with the Pen tool.

Figure 3.16 Drawing the profile of a skateboard using the Pen tool

4 Set the fill color to None and the stroke color to the Dark Violet swatch.

5 Open the Stroke panel and set the Weight to 1 pt and change the Cap setting to Round Cap.

Drawing the Skateboard Wheels

What's a skateboard without wheels? Next, you'll use the Ellipse tool to draw perfect circles under the skateboard deck you just created.

1 Using the Ellipse tool, Shift-drag to draw a circle beneath the skateboard deck profile. Make the circle about the size of a skateboard wheel.

2. If necessary, switch to the Selection tool and position the wheel at an appropriate location in relation to the skateboard deck. Set the fill color of the wheel to Dark Violet.

3. Using the Selection tool, copy the first wheel by Option-dragging (macOS) or Alt-dragging (Windows) the wheel to the right at an appropriate location.

4. Select the three objects that make up the skateboard and choose Object > Group to group the elements together (**Figure 3.17**).

Figure 3.17 The completed skateboard

Positioning the Skateboard on the Half-Pipe

Your skateboard may be beautifully drawn, but it doesn't generate any interest if it's just floating in space. Let's show it in motion in its native habitat!

1. Move the skateboard onto the half-pipe. Position the rear wheel (or the front if you prefer) so that it's just touching the surface of the half-pipe.

2. Select the Rotate tool 🔄 and click the edge of the wheel as shown in **Figure 3.18**. This establishes the point of transformation of the object using the Rotate tool.

Figure 3.18 Establishing the point of transformation

Figure 3.19 The skateboard rotated so that it appears to be rolling on the surface of the half-pipe

3. Now move the cursor to the other end of the skateboard and drag to rotate the skateboard. Rotate it until the other wheel is the same distance from the surface of the half-pipe as the first wheel. You can let go of your mouse if necessary, but if you want to continue rotating, you'll need to drag each time. If you simply click, you'll reestablish the point of transformation.

4. Using the Selection tool, fine-tune the position of the skateboard so that it looks convincing (**Figure 3.19**).

5. Save your document.

Congratulations! You've completed the front of the business card (**Figure 3.20**)! Feel free to tweak the design and make additional adjustments on your own.

Figure 3.20 The completed front of the business card

CHAPTER OBJECTIVES

Chapter Learning Objectives

- Draw, split, and join paths.
- Group and ungroup objects.
- Work in isolation mode.
- Use the Appearance panel.
- Create and work with graphic styles.
- Work with layers.
- Set type on a path.
- Create a pattern swatch.

Chapter ACA Objectives

For full descriptions of the objectives, see the table on pages 196–204.

DOMAIN 2.0
PROJECT SETUP AND INTERFACE
2.3d, 2.5, 2.5a, 2.5b, 2.5c, 2.6, 2.6a, 2.6b

DOMAIN 3.0
ORGANIZATION OF DOCUMENTS
3.1, 3.1a, 3.1b, 3.2b

DOMAIN 4.0
CREATE AND MODIFY VISUAL ELEMENTS
4.1a, 4.1b, 4.2, 4.3a, 4.3b, 4.3c, 4.4b, 4.5a, 4.5b, 4.5c, 4.6b, 4.6c

CHAPTER 4

Creating the Back of a Business Card

In this chapter, we'll create a new document for the back of the Session Skate Shop business card. Normally, however, it would make sense to add an additional artboard to the document containing the front of the card that we created in Chapter 3. If you'd like, you can follow along with the exercises in this chapter but do your work in an artboard that you add to the front of the card. That will give you a completed file. Or you can create a new file, as shown in the video. Throughout the chapter, we'll be creating a map of the area where the skate shop is located, and you'll learn techniques for drawing and manipulating paths and changing their appearance. The Appearance panel in Adobe Illustrator CC is incredibly powerful and allows you to create complex appearances from simple, basic paths.

★ *ACA Objective 4.1b*

★ *ACA Objective 4.5a*

★ *ACA Objective 4.5b*

▶ **Video 4.1** *Creating the Streets*

Drawing the Streets of the Map

To get started, you can create a new document based on one of the presets in the Print category of the New Document dialog box. Set the width to **3.5 in** and the height to **2 in** with a **.125 in** bleed. This is the size of a standard business card with bleed. Conversely, you can save a copy of the front of the business card that you created in Chapter 3 and simply add another artboard to the document using the same specifications. Normally we'd put both the front and the back of the business card in the same file, but for clarity in this book, and in the accompanying videos, we chose to create a new file.

With the file created or the artboard added, you can begin to draw the streets of the area where the skate shop is located. Feel free to follow along with the streets that are drawn in the video, or be creative and come up with your own street configuration for the business card. Keep in mind, however, that the streets that were drawn in the video were done in a way so that other techniques can be learned later in the chapter. So have fun and enjoy learning how to manipulate paths in Illustrator!

Drawing and Modifying Paths for the Streets

The first thing we'll do is draw a circle in the upper-left corner of the business card. This circle will represent a traffic circle on the map.

1   Using the Ellipse tool, Shift-drag to draw a perfect circle on the artboard.

2   Set the stroke color to black and the stroke weight to 5 pt.

Figure 4.1 Selecting the Scissors tool by clicking and holding the Eraser tool

Note that the traffic circle itself is not a complete circle. It's more like three quarters of a circle, so we'll need to cut the path to achieve the desired result. Illustrator has two powerful tools for splitting paths: the Knife tool and the Scissors tool . You can find both of these tools by pressing and holding the Eraser tool . (**Figure 4.1**).

The Knife tool affects only closed paths; drag across the object to cut the path. The result is two new closed paths. The Scissors tool, by comparison, can be used on both open and closed paths. Click the spot on the path where you want to cut it. If you clicked an open path, the result is two new open paths. If you use the Scissors tool on a closed path, the result is an open path.

1   Using the Scissors tool, click the ellipse in the lower-left portion of the circle to cut the path at that location.

2   Click again on the far right of the ellipse with the Scissors tool to cut the path at that location as well.

3   Press Delete (macOS) or Backspace (Windows) twice to delete the lower-right portion of the path (**Figure 4.2**). If you delete the wrong portion of the ellipse, choose Edit > Undo and then select the Direct Selection tool, click the correct portion of the path, and press Delete/Backspace.

Figure 4.2 After deleting a portion of the ellipse

The Line tool is ideal for drawing straight open paths in any direction. We'll add some streets extending from the ends of the traffic circle now by drawing a few paths with the Line tool.

1   Using the Line tool , drag from the lower-left open end of the ellipse down and to the left, extending the path past the bleed guide on the artboard.

2   Draw another line from the right open end of the ellipse and Shift-drag to the right, extending the line again past the bleed guide. Feel free to drag the line considerably past the bleed guide as we'll clip all the extra artwork later in this chapter.

Joining Paths

We want to join our straight street lines to the traffic circle shape (the ellipse). Illustrator offers several ways to join two ends of open paths together. One method is the Join command. To use the Join command, simply select the Direct Selection tool, select the anchor points on the ends of each path, and choose Object > Path > Join. For basic connections, the Join command is usually sufficient, but it's not particularly intelligent as it simply connects the two dots, not taking into account how two endpoints should join naturally based on their existing path shapes.

The Join tool is another method of joining two paths together, which you'll use to join the straight paths to the ellipse. The Join tool takes into account the shape of the paths being joined and attempts to create a more natural connection between the paths.

1   Select the Join tool ![join tool icon] from the Tools panel by clicking and holding on the Shaper tool.

2   Scrub with the mouse over the endpoints of two line segments where the ellipse and line meet. When you release the mouse, the two endpoints will be joined together (**Figure 4.3**).

3   Repeat step 2 for the other endpoints where the line segment and ellipse meet.

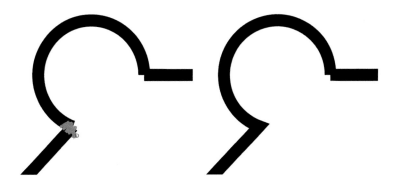

Figure 4.3 Scrubbing over two endpoints with the Join tool (left); the result (right)

Using the Line tool, continue drawing more straight lines to represent the cross streets as well as a diagonal street in the upper-right corner. Once again, you can follow along with Video 4.1, mimicking the streets drawn there, or you can get creative and draw your own streets.

Drawing Curved Streets

There are many ways to draw curved paths in Illustrator. You can use the Pen tool, but until you have some practice, using it can be a bit challenging. The Pencil tool is easy to use, because it allows you to use the natural movements of the mouse to generate a path. You can then further refine the path by using the Smooth tool .

1   Using the Pencil tool, draw a curved snake-like line that goes from the top left of the artboard down to the lower right of the artboard, as shown in the video (**Figure 4.4**).

Figure 4.4 Drawing a curved line using the Pencil tool

It can be difficult to draw smoothly using the mouse, so if you're not happy with the line that you've drawn, you can use the Smooth tool to smooth out the rough edges.

2   Using the Smooth tool, trace over the curved line that you drew in step 1 to remove extra anchor points and to smooth out the path. Feel free to do it more than once. Each time you drag over the path, it'll reshape and smooth the path accordingly.

3   Go ahead and draw another curved line extending from the angled path in the upper-right corner of the card down to the bottom middle of the card.

4   Draw two more curved lines that extend out from the traffic circle: one from the top of the circle to the upper-left corner of the card and another from the left side of the circle, down and to the left.

There are some areas of the card where the lines overlap other lines and extend too far into other areas. Follow along in the video and use the Eraser tool to remove those areas that extend too far and to tidy up the map in order to achieve the appearance you want.

Selecting Objects and Working with Groups

★ ACA Objective 2.3d

★ ACA Objective 4.3a

★ ACA Objective 4.3b

★ ACA Objective 4.3c

▶ **Video 4.2**
Selecting Based on Appearance and Working with Groups

When you're working with several design elements or objects in Illustrator, selecting the individual elements can be challenging. Next you'll learn techniques for selecting elements with similar properties. Grouping elements is a great way to connect elements so that when you select any of the objects within a **group**, they will all be included in the selection. In this next section, you'll learn how to select and group objects and then work with those existing groups.

Selecting and Grouping Objects

So far in our map, we have several streets that we've drawn that have a similar appearance. Although we could just choose Select > All, it won't always be that easy. Sometimes you can just select everything you want to work with in the document and go from there. More often than not, though, you want to select only certain items.

1   Select one of the lines (streets) in Illustrator using the Selection tool.

2   Choose Select > Same > Stroke Color. Notice that every object in the document that has a black stroke is now selected.

Notice under the Select > Same submenu, you have a number of choices for selecting objects based on different properties of the selected object. This makes it easy to adjust properties of items that have similar appearances.

Regardless of your selection method, if you select elements and you want to be able to select them again later without having to painstakingly select each

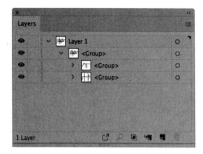

Figure 4.5 The Layers panel displays the structure of nested groups.

item all over again, you can choose Select > Save Selection and give the selection a name. Then, whenever you want those elements selected again in the future, just choose Select and choose the selection that you named (saved selections are listed at the bottom of the menu).

3 Click one of the curved paths with the Selection tool and then Shift-click the other curved paths to select all the curved paths in the map.

4 Choose Object > Group. All the selected objects are grouped together.

5 Click one of the straight paths with the Selection tool and then Shift-click the other straight paths. Choose Object > Group to group all the straight paths together into a single group.

6 Click any path in the original group and then Shift-click any path in the second group to select both groups at the same time. Choose Object > Group. This creates a nested group (groups inside of another group).

7 Open the Layers panel to get a better idea of how the groups are structured (**Figure 4.5**).

Working with Groups

Within the Layers panel, you can double-click the name of the group and enter a more appropriate name to make it easier to identify later. Either way, those groups will keep the items grouped together until you ungroup them by selecting the group and choosing Object > Ungroup. Although ungrouping elements works and it allows you to edit the items within the group, you'll probably have to regroup the elements again when you're finished if you want to keep those elements together.

TIP

Press Option (macOS) or Alt (Windows) with the Direct Selection tool to quickly access the Group Selection tool.

There are better ways to work with items in a group without having to ungroup them. One method is by using the Group Selection tool. Using the Group Selection tool, clicking an object will select it as you would expect to happen with the Direct Selection tool. If you click the object again, however, it will select the group of which the object is a member. Click again, and it will select the next group that the group is a member of (if it is a member of or nested within another group). Keep the Group Selection tool in mind when you need to work with elements of a group or nested groups.

ISOLATION MODE

One of the more underrated and often misunderstood features of Illustrator is isolation mode. Isolation mode provides a way of editing the contents of a group without having to ungroup the group.

1 Using the Selection tool, double-click an item on the artboard that you wish to edit. You'll notice a gray bar appear across the top of the document window called the isolation mode bar.

The isolation mode bar indicates that you've "drilled down" inside of a group and are now editing the contents of the group. Within the isolation mode bar, you'll see Layer 1 <Group> indicating that you're currently on layer 1 and editing the main group. This is where naming the groups can be very beneficial.

2 Click an item and you'll now select one of the groups nested within the main group. Double-click an item within one of the groups. The isolation mode bar changes to show you that you're now in Layer 1 <Group> <Group>, meaning that you're on Layer 1, editing the group that is nested within the main group.

You'll notice now, however, that you can click each item within the group that you're editing. Go ahead and move items around. Edit and adjust them; you can even switch tools to modify the elements to your liking. You'll notice that all the elements that are not within the group that you're editing are dimmed, meaning that they currently are not editable.

When you're finished editing, you can exit isolation mode by doing one of the following:

- Press the Escape key.
- Click the left arrow in the isolation mode bar until it disappears.
- Click the gray area of the isolation mode bar to the left of the named objects.
- Double-click the canvas or a blank area of the artboard.

Isolation mode is useful for more than just editing groups. This mode works with clipping masks and compound paths as well, which you'll learn more about in Chapter 5.

★ ACA Objective 2.6a

★ ACA Objective 2.6b

★ ACA Objective 4.5c

★ ACA Objective 4.6b

★ ACA Objective 4.6c

Using the Appearance Panel

Another incredibly powerful feature in Illustrator is the Appearance panel. The Appearance panel allows you to modify and add to the visual appearance of an object. For example, using the Appearance panel you can add multiple fills and multiple strokes, as well as various effects to a single object or path. In this example, we're going to make the streets look as if they have a stroke with a border, but in reality we're going to apply two strokes on top of each other.

▶ **Video 4.3** Using the Appearance Panel to Add an Appearance to the Streets

1   For simplicity, we'll start by ungrouping the objects from the previous section. Select the streets and choose Object > Ungroup. Now choose Object > Ungroup once again to ungroup the lower-level groups as well.

2   Using the Selection tool, select one of the streets (paths) on the map. Open the Appearance panel by choosing Window > Appearance.

    The Appearance panel will show Path at the top of the panel, indicating that a path is currently targeted, and the appearance of the targeted path will be indicated below. In this case we see a 5 pt black stroke and a fill of none.

3   At the bottom of the Appearance panel, click the Add New Stroke button ☐ to add a second stroke to the selected path.

    The stacking order of the items in the Appearance panel is the same as the stacking order of objects in a document. The topmost items will appear in front of the items below.

4   Select the bottom stroke in the Appearance panel and then click the stroke color and change it to cyan; then change the Weight value to **6 pt** (**Figure 4.6**).

Figure 4.6 Adding another stroke in the Appearance panel (left); the result (right)

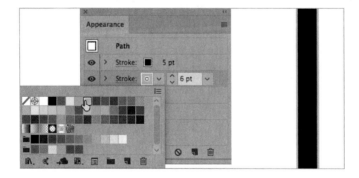

Creating a Graphic Style

You should now begin to see the power of the Appearance panel. We've added two different strokes of varying sizes to a single path. You can even add more strokes if you wish! Now that we've adjusted the appearance of one of the street elements and we're happy with the way that it looks, we now want to make the other street elements look the same. Although we could individually select all the other streets, we're going to use another amazing Illustrator feature called *graphic styles*. Graphic styles are essentially sets of Appearance panel properties that you save so that all of those properties can be reapplied to other objects quickly and easily.

1   Begin by selecting the object that you applied the appearance attributes to in the previous section.

2   Open the Graphic Styles panel by choosing Window > Graphic Styles. By default, the Graphic Styles panel contains a few graphic styles that you can apply to objects.

3   Drag the selected object that contains the appearance attributes and drop it on the Graphic Styles panel (**Figure 4.7**). You'll notice a new style has been added to the panel.

4   Double-click the new graphic style that you created, and in the Graphic Style Options dialog box, change Style Name to **Streets** and click OK (**Figure 4.8**).

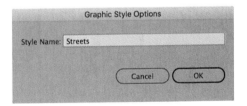

Figure 4.8 Renaming the graphic style in the Graphic Style Options dialog box

Figure 4.7 Dragging an object into the Graphic Styles panel and dropping it to create a new graphic style

With the new graphic style created and the path still selected, you'll notice that the top of the Appearance panel shows Path:Streets, which indicates that the selected path has the Streets graphic style applied to it. The Appearance panel will always provide a behind-the-scenes view of what is actually applied to the selected object(s).

1 Choose Select > All to select all of the paths in the document.

NOTE

If you decided to add a new artboard to the business card front document, choosing Select > All will also select everything on the front of the business card. To select only the streets on the back of the business card, simply use the Selection tool to drag across all the street paths or choose Select > All On Active Artboard.

2 In the Graphic Styles panel, click the Streets graphic style to apply the appearance attributes defined within to the selected paths of the streets.

Notice that all of the streets are now formatted using the same appearance attributes defined in the graphic style (**Figure 4.9**).

Figure 4.9 Applying the graphic style to all of the paths on the back of the business card.

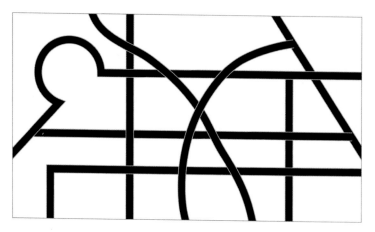

Updating a Graphic Style

One of the powerful aspects of a graphic style is that you can adjust the appearance of all objects with a graphic style applied by updating the graphic style. This allows you to make appearance changes to objects in a document with just a couple of clicks!

1 With the Selection tool, select one of the street paths on the back of the business card.

2. Open the Swatches panel, and open the Swatch Libraries menu found in the lower-left corner of the Swatches panel (**Figure 4.10**).

3. Choose Other Library and then navigate to the file that you saved for the front of the business card and click Open. All the swatches from that other file will appear in a new panel.

4. Click the folder icon to the left of all the swatches that you just displayed in the new panel to add those swatches to the Swatches panel of the business card back file. Close the panel that you opened in step 3 since you no longer need it.

5. Apply the lavender swatch (third from the left) to the top stroke in the Appearance panel, and apply the black swatch to the bottom stroke. Feel free to use any of the colors that you'd like to use for the street colors.

6. Open the Graphic Styles panel, and while holding Option (macOS) or Alt (Windows), drag the path that contains the new appearance and drop it on top of the graphic style in the Graphic Styles panel (**Figure 4.11**). You'll notice a border appear around the graphic style, indicating that you're updating that graphic style.

Figure 4.10 Loading a color library from the Swatches panel Swatch Libraries menu

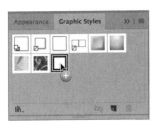

Figure 4.11 Updating a graphic style by Option-dragging (macOS) or Alt-dragging (Windows) an object onto an existing graphic style

Notice that after you update the graphic style, every object with that graphic style updates to match the new appearance of the object being used to update the graphic style. Alternatively, you can also update a graphic style by choosing Redefine Graphic Style "Streets" from the Appearance panel menu.

Working with Layers

★ *ACA Objective 3.1*

★ *ACA Objective 3.1a*

★ *ACA Objective 3.1b*

★ *ACA Objective 4.3a*

★ *ACA Objective 4.6b*

Before we create additional layers for the back of the business card, there are a few details to add first. There's one street that protrudes beyond the diagonal street in the upper-right corner of the card. That street needs to end where it meets the diagonal street. So, using your tool of choice, cut the path so that it abuts the diagonal line, as shown in **Figure 4.12**. The video uses the Eraser tool, but you can use any tool that you wish.

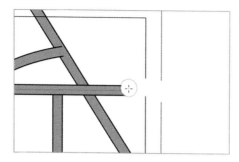

Figure 4.12 Using the Eraser tool to remove the excess length from the overlapping path

▶ Video 4.4
Organizing the Content on the Back of the Card Using Layers

Next we'll draw a shape that represents a grassy area on the map.

1 Begin by drawing a rectangle just big enough to cover the triangular area of the card in the upper-right corner and extend it beyond the edge of the artboard. Don't extend the rectangle beyond the diagonal line any more than necessary.

2 Give the new rectangle a stroke of None and fill with a green color to represent a grassy area. Use whatever green color you wish, and create a new swatch from that color and name it **Grass Green**.

3 Select the green rectangle and the diagonal path using the Selection tool.

4 Select the Shape Builder tool 🔧 , and while holding Option (macOS) or Alt (Windows), click the lower-left corner of the rectangle to remove that part of the rectangle (**Figure 4.13**).

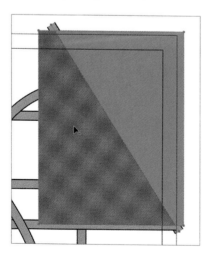

Figure 4.13 Using the Shape Builder tool to remove the lower-left portion of the rectangle

The Layers Panel

We'll now begin to organize the elements on the back of the business card using layers. Layers help to isolate and manage the objects in the document, making it easier to control them. The Layers panel shows you the stacking order (depth order) of the objects in a document. Just as objects have a stacking order in a document, so too do the layers themselves.

1. Open the Layers panel by choosing Window > Layers.

2. Double-click Layer 1 and rename the layer **Streets**. Press Return (macOS)/Enter (Windows) to commit the change.

3. Option-click (macOS) or Alt-click (Windows) the Create New Layer button ![icon] to create a new layer and display the Layer Options dialog box so that you can name the layer while you create it. Type **Landmarks** in the Name field and click OK.

4. Drag the Landmarks layer below the Streets layer to change the stacking order of the layers (**Figure 4.14**).

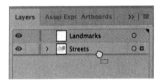

Figure 4.14 Dragging the Landmarks layer below the Streets layer

With the layers created and the stacking order of the layers in place, you're now ready to begin organizing the elements on the card onto their appropriate layers. At this point, all of the objects in the file are on the Streets layer since that is the original layer that we started with. We've created the Landmarks layer, but currently it's empty.

1. Using the Selection tool, select the green triangle in the upper-right corner of the card.

   Notice that in the Layers panel, there's a small blue square at the far right side of the Streets layer. That blue square is in the Layers panel *selection column* and indicates that the selected object is currently on the Streets layer.

2. Drag the blue square down and drop it on the Landmarks layer (**Figure 4.15**).

Figure 4.15 Moving the green triangle object from the Streets layer to the Landmarks layer by dragging the square at the right side of the Layers panel

   You'll notice a few things happen as soon as you let go of the mouse button. The square is now on the Landmarks layer and the bounding box around the green triangle, as well as the path that makes up the triangle, is now red because the Landmarks layer was assigned the red color by default when it was created.

The card is really taking shape! However, the streets on the map now overlap one another, which is not how those streets actually look. This is because we've applied the graphic style to each individual object, so each object has its own separate appearance. In the next steps, we'll adjust that to make the lines intersect the way that streets actually should appear.

1. In the Layers panel, click the far right of the Streets layer to select all of the paths on that layer.

2. In the Appearance panel, choose Clear Appearance from the panel menu. This removes any appearance attributes from the selected objects, essentially setting the stroke and fill to none (**Figure 4.16**).

Figure 4.16 Clearing the appearance attributes of the selected object

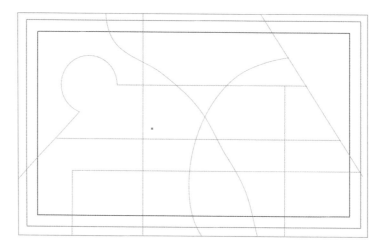

TIP

Targeting and selecting are very similar. Using the Appearance panel to target an object also selects the object and selecting an object also targets it. However, you can only target a layer using the Layers panel by clicking the target icon (see "Working with Layers" later in this chapter).

3. In the Layers panel again, click the small circle (the target icon) to the right of the Streets layer (in the *targeting and appearance column* of the Layers panel) to target the objects on the layer (**Figure 4.17**).

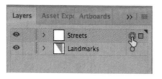

Figure 4.17 Clicking the target icon to target the entire Streets layer

4. In the Graphic Styles panel, click the Streets graphic style to apply the graphic style to the entire layer this time instead of the individual paths (streets). You'll notice the circle changes from a hollow circle to a filled circle to indicate that the layer now has appearance attributes applied.

Notice that the street intersections show a more natural merging of the paths because the style is applied to the entire layer as a whole instead of the individual paths (**Figure 4.18**). Any path that you now draw on the Streets layer will inherit the appearance attributes applied to the layer, making the process of adding more streets to the map incredibly easy and efficient. Understanding the concept of targeting will give you the ability to harness the power of Illustrator when creating your own designs.

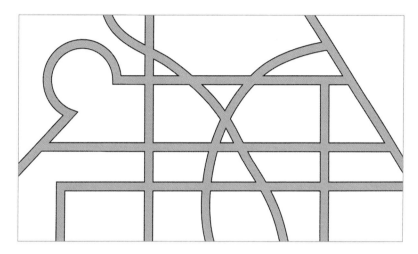

Figure 4.18 Applying the graphic style to the layer

Adding Names to the Streets on the Map

★ ACA Objective 4.2

For ease of navigation, it's helpful to identify each street on the map by name. To do this, we'll add text objects to the map and position them appropriately on each street. Now obviously this is a fictitious map, so don't think that you need to use the same names that were used in the video. You're a creative person! Use whatever names you wish and have fun with your map!

▶ **Video 4.5** Adding Names to Each Street on the Map

1   Begin by creating a new layer in the Layers panel and name that layer **Street Names**. Make sure that this layer is the topmost layer in the Layers panel because we want the street names to appear on top of all the other elements of the card.

2   With the Street Names layer active, click anywhere on the card using the Type tool to create a new point type object on the card. Now type the name of your first street. In the video we used **Franklin Street**, but you can use whatever name you prefer.

3 We need the text to fit within the bounds of the street, so using the Properties, Control, or Character panel, change the font and size of the text to something that looks appropriate. In the video we used Myriad Pro at 6 pt. Position the text on top of one of the streets.

4 Using the Selection tool, hold down Option (macOS) or Alt (Windows) and drag the text object to make a copy. Type a new name for the copy of the street and position it over a different street.

5 Repeat the previous steps until you have a name for all of the horizontal, vertical, and diagonal streets on the card (**Figure 4.19**).

Figure 4.19 Adding the names to the streets of the card

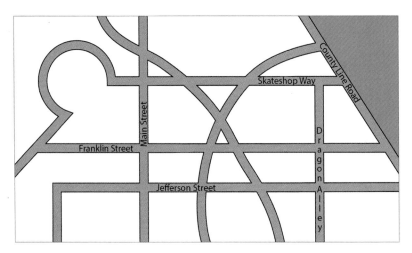

Setting Type on a Path

For the curved roads of the map, type in a straight line just doesn't work. We want the text to follow the shape of the path for each road so that each is properly labeled with text that's easy to read.

1 Using the Selection tool, select the two curved streets on the map.

2 While holding down Option (macOS) or Alt (Windows), drag the square at the right end of the Streets layer and drop it on the Street Names layer. This makes a copy of the selected objects on the Street Names layer (**Figure 4.20**).

Figure 4.20 Moving copies of the curved streets onto the Street Names layer

3   Select one of the copied curved paths to make it active. Now, using the Type On A Path tool 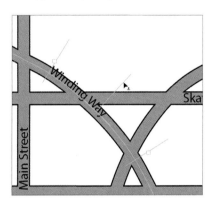, click the selected curved path to convert it to a **path type** object and to apply default text to the path.

4   Begin typing a new street name to replace the default text. Note that the text follows the shape of the path.

5   To adjust the location of the type on the path, switch to the Selection tool and drag the bracket at the end of the path toward the text to shorten the type on the path object (**Figure 4.21**). Then drag the middle bracket to slide the type along the path to a new location

NOTE

After adding type on a path, you may want the type oriented to the other side of the path. To flip the type over the path, use the Selection tool to drag the middle bracket across the path.

Figure 4.21 Moving the type along the path by dragging the bracket

6   To adjust how the text aligns to the path, select the text using the Type On a Path tool and then adjust the baseline shift value in the Character panel.

7   Repeat the previous steps to add a name to the other curved street on the map, and then save the file.

★ ACA Objective 2.5c

★ ACA Objective 2.6a

Creating and Applying a Pattern Swatch

★ ACA Objective 2.6b

★ ACA Objective 4.4b

▶ **Video 4.6** Creating a Pattern Swatch for the Landmarks

For the landmark areas of the business card, we'll add a **pattern** to give those elements more visual interest and to represent the grassy areas on the map. Although you could manually draw the texture of the pattern each time, patterns save you a lot of time and provide powerful control over the appearance of those items.

1   Make sure the Landmarks layer is active and begin by drawing a circle using the Ellipse tool. Position the circle inside the traffic circle in the upper-left corner of the card.

This ellipse represents a grassy area inside the traffic circle. You'll now create a pattern to fill this and another grassy area on the card.

2   Make sure that no object is currently selected, and then choose Object > Pattern > Make. A dialog box opens, alerting you that a new pattern has been added to the Swatches panel. Click OK.

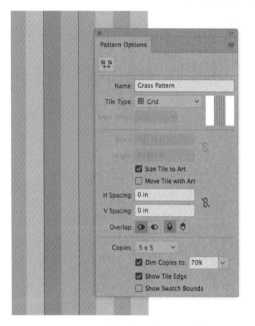

At this point you are in Pattern Editing mode, as indicated by the isolation mode bar at the top of the screen. Anything you draw in this mode will become part of the pattern.

3   Using the Line tool, draw a vertical line from the top to the bottom of the pattern tile. Set the stroke weight to 4 pt and the color to green.

4   With the line selected, choose Edit > Copy and then choose Edit > Paste In Front to paste a copy of the line directly on top of the original.

5   Move the line 4 points to the right of the original line by selecting the copy, opening the Transform panel, typing **+4 pt** after the current value in the X field, and pressing Return/Enter. Change the color of the duplicated object to a lighter shade of the original green color.

6   In the Pattern Options panel, enable the Size Tile To Art check box to resize the tile to the size of the artwork.

Figure 4.22 Resizing the tile to the artwork by selecting the Size Tile To Art check box

7   Enter **Grass Pattern** for the name (**Figure 4.22**).

8   Exit Pattern Editing mode by pressing the Esc key on your keyboard. (The pattern will be saved in the Swatches panel.)

Applying the Pattern to the Grassy Areas of the Map

Once a pattern is created, you can apply it to any object that you wish. A pattern swatch behaves like any other swatch in Illustrator. It can be applied to the fill or stroke of an object.

1 Select the ellipse in the middle of the traffic circle.

2 Select the fill of the object and select the pattern swatch in the Swatches panel that you just created. The ellipse is filled with the striped pattern.

3 To scale the pattern within the ellipse, do one of the following:

- Double-click the Scale tool and deselect Transform Objects and select Transform Patterns. Type a scale value in one or more of the scale fields and click OK (**Figure 4.23**).

- With the Scale tool selected, hold down the tilde key (~) on your keyboard and drag to scale only the pattern and not the object. Add the Shift key to scale proportionally.

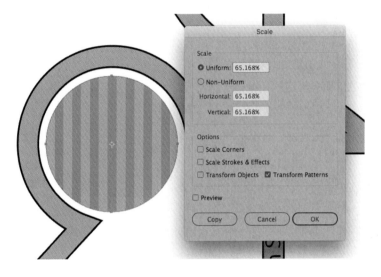

Figure 4.23 Scaling the pattern by double-clicking the Scale tool

Adding a Gradient Effect and Details to the Landmarks

Now that we have a pattern applied to the ellipse in the traffic circle, we'll refine it a bit by adding some shading to it. We'll accomplish this using a combination of a gradient fill and a useful blending mode. Feel free to experiment with the options to see what other creative effects you can come up with.

1 With the ellipse selected, open the Appearance panel and add a new fill to the shape by clicking the Add New Fill button at the bottom left of the panel.

★ ACA Objective 2.5

★ ACA Objective 2.5a

★ ACA Objective 2.5b

★ ACA Objective 2.5c

★ ACA Objective 4.1a

★ ACA Objective 4.5a

★ ACA Objective 4.5c

Video 4.7 *Adding a Gradient Effect to the Landmarks*

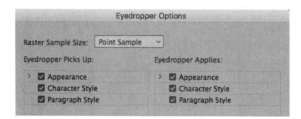

Figure 4.24 Adjusting the blending mode and opacity of the gradient

2   Open the Gradient panel by choosing Window > Gradient, and choose Radial from the Type menu. A default black to white gradient is added to the ellipse.

3   The Gradient ramp shows you the color stops, which indicate what colors make up the gradient, and you can drag them as well as the transition point to adjust how the gradient is composed. You can also, of course, change the colors used to create the gradient.

4   Open the Transparency panel by choosing Window > Transparency and choose Multiply from the Blending Mode menu. Multiply is one of the easiest blending modes to understand, because it multiplies the color of the object with the color underneath it.

5   If desired, adjust the opacity of the gradient to change the intensity (**Figure 4.24**).

Applying the Grass Appearance to Other Objects Using the Eyedropper Tool

Earlier in this chapter, you used the Graphic Styles panel to create a graphic style to apply to other objects. This is a powerful way to reapply appearance attributes to other objects, but when you just need to apply those attributes to one or two objects, you might decide to use the capabilities of the Eyedropper tool as well.

1   Using the Selection tool, select the green triangle in the upper-right corner of the business card.

2   Double-click the Eyedropper tool in the Tools panel to open the Eyedropper Options dialog box.

    In the Eyedropper Options dialog box, you can choose which attributes you want to pick up using the Eyedropper tool and which attributes you want to apply using the Eyedropper tool. Depending on your design, you may want to change the properties being picked up and applied to other objects.

3   In the Eyedropper Options dialog box, enable all three of the major categories to pick up and apply. Click OK (**Figure 4.25**).

Figure 4.25 Selecting options in the Eyedropper Options dialog box

4   Using the Eyedropper tool, click the ellipse that has the pattern and gradient applied. Because the triangle was selected, the attributes of the ellipse are now also applied to the triangle.

Adding the Pond

In the center of the traffic circle, there's also a pond-like water area that needs to be added to the card. Feel free to make this water area any shape that you like, or you can follow along with the video to replicate what was done there.

1   Make sure that the Landmark layer is active in the Layers panel and select the Blob Brush tool ![icon]. You'll find this tool by clicking and holding on the Brush tool.

2   In the Swatches panel, choose a blue color to represent the color of the water.

3   To change the brush size, you can press the [or] key on your keyboard to make the brush smaller or larger.

4   Start painting in the middle of the ellipse to draw the shape of the water area. If you let go of the mouse, Illustrator completes drawing of the path, but you can just click again to add to the shape. To ensure that you're adding to the shape, you may want to select the shape first before continuing to draw.

5   If you'd like to smooth the shape, choose Object > Path > Simplify and adjust the curve precision and angle threshold to control how much adjustment is applied.

Finishing Up: Adding Symbols and Trimming the Artwork

To finish up the back of the business card, we'll add some icons that represent key areas on the map. To do this, we'll use symbols. Symbols contain several benefits when working in Illustrator, the main benefit of which is that any symbol instance added in the file will update if any changes are ever made to the symbol.

Before we go too far, if you'd like to add a color to the background of the business card, go ahead and create a new layer at the bottom of the stacking order and draw a rectangle that encompasses the artboard using the color of your choice.

★ *ACA Objective 2.6*

★ *ACA Objective 2.6a*

★ *ACA Objective 2.6b*

★ *ACA Objective 3.2b*

▶ *Video 4.8 Adding the Finishing Touches to the Map on the Back of the Business Card*

Creating a Symbol

1   Create a new layer called **Locations**. This will serve as a place for the icons representing the key locations you'll be putting on the card. Position this layer at the top of the stacking order in the Layers panel and keep this layer active for the next step.

2   Using the Star tool ☆, drag to draw a star on the artboard where you'd like a key feature represented on the map. For now you can leave the stroke set to None and the fill set to black.

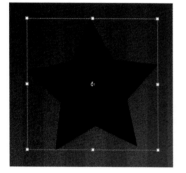

3   Open the Symbols panel by choosing Window > Symbols, and drag the star shape you drew in step 1 onto the Symbols panel. The Symbol Options dialog box appears.

4   Enter **Key Location** in the Name field and click OK.

The type of symbol doesn't really matter when you're designing for a print product. If you were creating art that would be used for the web or repurposed in an animation program like Adobe Animate CC, then you might want to adjust the symbol settings.

5   In the Symbols panel, drag the Key Location symbol onto the artboard. You've just created a symbol instance. Symbol instances are identified by a small icon in the middle (**Figure 4.26**).

Figure 4.26 A symbol instance represented by an icon in the middle of the symbol

Modifying a Symbol

The benefit of using symbols is that each symbol instance that you create by dragging from the Symbols panel is connected to that original symbol. So any updates you make to the symbol itself will be reflected in all of the symbol instances in the document.

1   In the Symbols panel, double-click the Key Location symbol. You are taken into Symbol Editing mode.

2   Scale the star shape down a bit and change the fill color to white.

3   Press the Esc key on the keyboard to exit Symbol Editing mode and notice that each instance of the Key Location symbol updates to match the edit that you made to the symbol.

Using Symbol Libraries

When constructing a map, one of the challenges can be to produce all the different graphics you need to represent the various types of landmarks in the area covered by the map. It would be a real time-saver if you had access to a collection of pre-built graphics designed for maps. You're in luck! Illustrator provides whole libraries of symbols for a wide variety of purposes.

1   Click the Symbol Libraries button ▊▊ at the bottom of the Symbols panel to open a menu listing the libraries of symbols that ship with Illustrator (**Figure 4.27**).

2   Choose Maps from the menu. The Maps symbol library opens in a separate panel (**Figure 4.28**).

3   Drag some symbols from the library panel to the artboard and try them out in your design. Add text if needed.

Tons of great symbols that can be used as artwork in your projects are easily available for you to use.

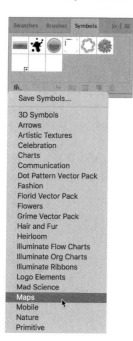

Figure 4.27 ◄ Loading the Maps symbol library from the Symbol Libraries menu on the Symbols panel

Figure 4.28 ▲ Once loaded, the Maps symbol library opens in its own panel.

Using a Clipping Mask to trim the Artwork

Our final task is to delete the bits of artwork that extend beyond the bleed. To do that, we'll use a rectangle on a new top layer as a clipping mask.

1 Choose View > Smart Guides to activate Smart Guides again.

2 In the Layers panel, create a new layer at the top of the layer stack. Give it the name **Clip**.

3 Select the Rectangle tool and drag in the Clip layer to draw a rectangle. Make sure the bounds of the rectangle snap to the bleed guide (**Figure 4.29**).

Figure 4.29 Drawing a rectangle to serve as a clipping mask

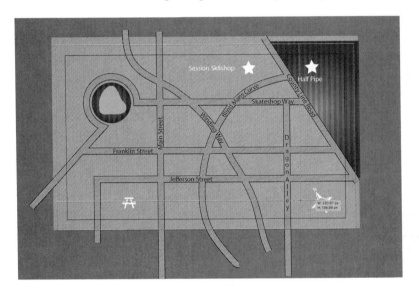

4 Fill the rectangle with white (this is a temporary color, just to make the rectangle easier to see).

5 In the Layers panel, click the disclosure triangle on the Clip layer to open it and display the Rectangle object.

6 Click the Locations layer to select it, then hold Shift and click the Background layer.

All of the layers below the Clip layer are now selected.

7 Drag the selected layers up and slightly to the right. Release the mouse when a dark line appears under the Rectangle object.

The selected layers are now sublayers of the Clip layer (**Figure 4.30**).

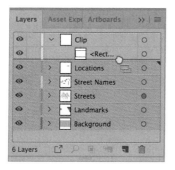

Figure 4.30 Dragging a stack of selected layers into the Clip layer beneath the Rectangle object (left) converts those layer to sublayers of the Clip layer (right).

8   Select the Clip layer and then click the Make/Release Clipping Mask button . The Rectangle object clips all of the elements beneath the Clip layer, acting as a clipping mask (**Figure 4.31**).

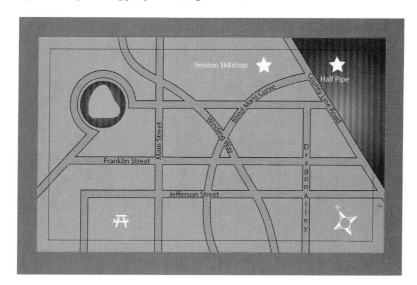

Figure 4.31 The clipping mask trims the graphic elements so they don't extend beyond the bleed guide.

9   Save your file.

Congratulations! You've completed the back of the business card! You can combine the artboards containing the front and back of the card into a single file and you'll have a complete business card, ready for printing.

CHAPTER OBJECTIVES

Chapter Learning Objectives

- Place images in Illustrator.
- Use the Pen tool.
- Duplicate and transform objects.
- Create a clipping mask.
- Create, apply, and edit a brush.
- Use Image Trace.
- Use envelope distort.
- Add effects.
- Package a project.

Chapter ACA Objectives

For full descriptions of the objectives, see the table on pages 196–204.

DOMAIN 1.0
WORKING IN THE DESIGN INDUSTRY
1.5b

DOMAIN 2.0
PROJECT SETUP AND INTERFACE
2.3c, 2.4a, 2.4b, 2.6

DOMAIN 3.0
ORGANIZATION OF DOCUMENTS
3.1, 3.1a, 3.1b, 3.2, 3.2a, 3.2b

DOMAIN 4.0
CREATE AND MODIFY VISUAL ELEMENTS
4.1a, 4.1b, 4.2, 4.2e, 4.3c, 4.4b, 4.5, 4.5b, 4.5d, 4.6a

DOMAIN 5.0
PUBLISHING DIGITAL MEDIA
5.2d

CHAPTER 5

Creating a Music Festival Poster

In this chapter you'll create a poster for a music festival that will be hung in local storefronts, posted in public locations, and collected by locals as souvenirs of the event. This project will allow you to dig deep into your creativity while you learn new techniques in Adobe Illustrator CC. You'll start by using a photograph as a reference for the artwork you'll be drawing, and then you'll add graphic elements to the poster to create the finished product. You're encouraged to have fun here and experiment with the techniques that you'll be introduced to. You don't have to match what was shown in the video exactly; add your own creative flair!

Placing an Image in Adobe Illustrator

★ ACA Objective 2.4a

★ ACA Objective 2.4b

▶ **Video 5.1** *Creating the Poster and Placing an Image*

We'll begin by creating a new document in Illustrator to the specifications of the poster that we're creating.

1   With Illustrator open, choose File > New or click the Create New button from the Start workspace to display the New Document dialog box.

2   Click the Print category at the top of the dialog box to view all presets based on the Print profile.

PRESET DETAILS

Music Poster

Width

| 18 in | Inches | ⌄ |

Height   Orientation   Artboards

| 24 in | ⌃⌄ 1 |

Bleed

Top   Bottom

| ⌃⌄ 0.125 in | ⌃⌄ 0.125 in |

Left   Right

| ⌃⌄ 0.125 in | ⌃⌄ 0.125 in | 🔗 |

⌄ Advanced Options

Color Mode

| CMYK Color | ⌄ |

Raster Effects

| High (300 ppi) | ⌄ |

Preview Mode

| Default | ⌄ |

Figure 5.1 Creating a new document to the specifications of the poster

Figure 5.2 Sizing the placed image on the Illustrator artboard

3 Change the units to inches and enter **18** in the Width field and **24** in the Height field. Set the bleed value for all sides of the document to **.125"**, and then click the Create button (**Figure 5.1**).

4 Choose File > Save and save the document as Music Poster.ai.

With the new document created, you'll now place an image to use as a reference.

1 Choose File > Place to open the Place dialog box.

2 In the exercise files folder that you downloaded for this course, select the Guitar.psd image. Click the Options button at the bottom of the window and select Link checkbox; then click Place. Your cursor will change to a loaded graphics pointer (sometimes called the "place gun") indicating that Illustrator is ready to place and position the image in the document.

When placing an image, you can choose to link to the image by selecting Link or you can embed the image by deselecting the option. Linking creates a reference to the original image file on your hard drive or server and keeps track of its location. Embedding, on the other hand, copies the entire image file into the Illustrator file, making it no longer dependent on the original file. Although embedding increases the size of the Illustrator file and makes it difficult to edit the image in the future, it is necessary for some tasks in Illustrator such as creating a brush from an image.

3 Drag to place and size the guitar image roughly to the size that you would like to use the image. Don't worry about getting it perfect. You'll tweak the size in the next steps.

If you were to just click with the loaded graphics pointer, Illustrator would place the image at 100% size. This is often much bigger than desired, so dragging instead of simply clicking will allow you to size the image roughly the way you want it.

4 Adjust the size of the image by dragging the handles of the image while holding down the Shift key on your keyboard to scale the image proportionally (**Figure 5.2**).

Creating a Template Layer

The placed image won't actually appear in the final poster. Instead, we'll use it as a reference for artwork that we'll draw in Illustrator. To facilitate this process, we'll create a template layer that is locked so that we can easily draw and manipulate artwork without inadvertently selecting or moving anything on the template layer.

1   Open the Layers panel by choosing Window > Layers or by clicking the Layers button in the panel dock.

2   The placed image is on Layer 1 since that's the default layer in all new Illustrator files, so we'll just rename that layer by double-clicking to the right of the Layer 1 name to display the Layer Options dialog box.

3   In the Layer Options dialog box, enter **Template** in the Name field, make sure the value in the Dim Images To field is 50% (the default), and select the option. Finally, select the Template option. Click OK.

    By converting a layer to a template layer, you have locked the layer. If the Dim Images To option has been selected, the images on that layer are dimmed or ghosted.

★ ACA Objective 3.1

★ ACA Objective 4.1b

★ ACA Objective 4.5

Drawing the Body of the Guitar

▶ **Video 5.2** *Using the Pen Tool to Draw the Shape of the Guitar*

We'll use the raster-based guitar image on our template layer as a guide for the vector-based drawing we'll create next. Some parts of the guitar lend themselves to being recreated by standard geometric shapes (the guitar's neck is close to a rectangle, for example). But the body of the guitar itself is irregular, and consists of several complex curves. That's just the sort of challenge the Pen tool was made to conquer!

Creating a New Layer

The only layer available in the Illustrator document at this point is the template layer, which is locked. We need to create a new layer that will contain the artwork that we're about to draw.

1   Open the Layers panel by clicking the Layers button in the panel dock or by choosing Window > Layers.

2   Option-click (macOS) or Alt-click (Windows) the Create New Layer button ▩ at the bottom of the Layers panel to display the Layer Options dialog box.

3   Enter **Guitar** in the Name field and leave the rest of the options at their default settings; then click OK.

Drawing with the Pen Tool

The Pen tool is arguably one of the most powerful yet challenging tools to use in Illustrator and other Adobe applications as well. It is the most accurate way to draw precisely using a mouse. That being said, you will not become a Pen tool master overnight. It requires practice and a bit of patience, but once you grasp the power of the Pen tool, you'll have amazing control when creating artwork in Illustrator.

1 Select the Pen tool  from the Tools panel.

2 Click the Guitar layer in the Layers panel to ensure that the artwork that you draw will appear on this layer.

3 Begin drawing on the upper-left edge of the guitar. Position the mouse pointer, press the mouse button to place an anchor point, and drag to the right. Use the anchor point references shown in **Figure 5.3** to guide you as you add more anchor points. The square points indicate where to click for the anchor points, and the round points indicate where to drag immediately after placing the anchor points.

4 When you come around to the beginning of the path again, hold down the Option key (macOS) or the Alt key (Windows) as you press the mouse button on the original anchor point and drag to finish the last line segment of the path. Using this modifier key provides control when finishing the path.

5 Adjust the path as necessary by following along with the video. Use the Command key (macOS) or the Ctrl key (Windows) to select anchor points and adjust both direction handles connected to each anchor point. Use the Option key (macOS) or the Alt key (Windows) to adjust individual direction handles for each line segment.

Figure 5.3 Drawing the body of the guitar using the Pen tool

6 With the path selected, click the fill indicator at the bottom of the Tools panel or in the Swatches panel, and use the Eyedropper tool to Shift-click the guitar image to fill the active path with the color that you pick up with the Eyedropper tool (**Figure 5.4**).

Figure 5.4 Shift-clicking the image (left) to fill the active path with the color picked up from the image (right)

Drawing the Neck of the Guitar

The neck of the guitar is a symmetrical object, so it doesn't make sense to draw this element freehand. Instead, you'll start with a basic shape and then adjust it to match the shape of the neck of the guitar.

1   Using the Rectangle tool, drag to draw a rectangle that encompasses the base of the guitar neck and extends up to the top of the guitar neck (**Figure 5.5**).

2   Using the Direct Selection tool ▷, click the anchor point in the upper-right corner of the rectangle; then Shift-click the anchor point in the upper left corner of the rectangle so that both anchor points are selected.

3   Using the Scale tool ⊡, click once at the bottom middle of the guitar neck to define the point of transformation. Now, click to the right or left of the selected anchor points and drag toward the neck of the guitar to scale the top of the neck of the guitar to make it narrower at the top (**Figure 5.6**).

4   Name the object in the layers panel for easy identification and fill the object with 90% black.

Figure 5.5 Drag with the Rectangle tool to draw the neck of the guitar.

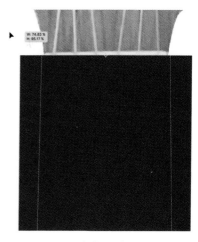

Figure 5.6 With the anchor points selected, click to the left and drag to the right to scale the top of the rectangle.

★ *ACA Objective 2.3c*

★ *ACA Objective 3.1a*

★ *ACA Objective 3.1b*

★ *ACA Objective 4.4b*

▶ **Video 5.3** *Drawing the Frets and Fret Markers on the Guitar*

Adding the Frets and Fret Markers to the Neck of the Guitar

The body and neck of the guitar are starting to come along, but we need more detail to make the guitar look realistic and recognizable. To do this, we'll add the frets to the guitar as well as the fret markers along with a few other details. It's important to remember in this section, as well as others, that there are many ways to achieve the same result. Throughout your creative career, you'll be judged on *what* you create, not *how* you create it. So keep this in mind as you learn new techniques, and if you find them useful, apply them to your own work.

Drawing the Frets and Marker Dots

To draw the frets, we'll continue working on the Guitar layer that we created earlier in this chapter. We'll add the artwork that we're about to create to that layer.

1. Hide the guitar neck and guitar body objects by clicking the visibility icons next to those objects in the Layers panel.

2. Using the Line tool ✐ , hold down the Shift key and drag a line across the top fret in the guitar image in the Template layer.

3. In the Stroke panel or Control panel, increase the stroke weight to about 3 pt and change the stroke color to 10% black.

4. Using the Selection tool, hold down Option (macOS) or Alt (Windows) and drag to make a copy of the line. While dragging, add the Shift key to keep the copy of the line aligned with the original line (**Figure 5.7**). Repeat for all of the frets on the neck of the guitar.

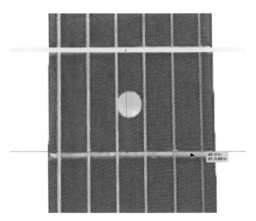

Figure 5.7 Making a copy of the line for each fret on the neck of the guitar

There are also marker dots on the neck of the guitar that are seen on virtually every guitar in one shape or another. In the case of our reference image, they are small circles that appear along the length of the neck. We'll replicate these marker dots using circles drawn with the Ellipse tool.

1. Navigate back to the top of the guitar neck, and using the Ellipse tool, draw a circle (hold down the Shift key) to the size of the topmost marker dot. If desired, use the Align panel to align the dot to one of the fret markers to keep the elements aligned. Fill the shape with 10% black.

2. Using the Selection tool, hold down Option (macOS) or Alt (Windows) and drag the ellipse down to the next marker dot on the fretboard to make a copy at that location. Repeat this for the remainder of the marker dots on the fretboard.

Clipping the Marker Dots and Frets to the Neck of the Guitar

Right now, the frets are extending beyond the edge of the neck of the guitar. This won't work for our finished product, so we'll use the shape that we drew for the fretboard to clip the frets and marker dots.

1. Make the Guitar Neck layer visible by clicking the visibility icon in the Layers panel.

2. Select the shape for the neck of the guitar and choose Object > Arrange > Bring To Front, or drag it above all the other artwork items in the Layers panel.

3. Using the Selection tool, create a marquee selection around the entire area of the fretboard to include the fretboard, frets, and marker dots (**Figure 5.8**).

4. Choose Object > Clipping Mask > Make. The frets and marker dots are now clipped to the frontmost shape.

When you create a clipping mask, you lose the fill color of the frontmost object. We'll add that back in the next step.

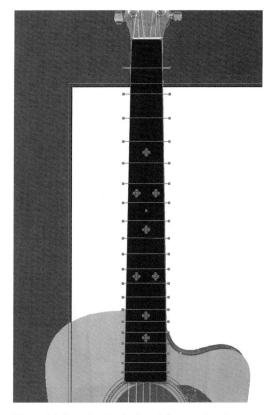

Figure 5.8 Selecting the fretboard, frets, and marker dots by marqueeing the area with the Selection tool

5 Using the Direct Selection tool, click the edge of the shape of the fretboard and apply the 90% black swatch to the fill of the object.

6 Using the Ellipse tool, hold down Shift and drag to draw a perfect circle over the sound hole of the guitar. While holding down the mouse as you draw the circle, you can temporarily hold down the spacebar to reposition the ellipse for proper positioning and alignment to the sound hole on the image. Fill this shape with a slightly darker color than was applied to the guitar body.

★ ACA Objective 1.5b

★ ACA Objective 2.6

★ ACA Objective 3.1a

★ ACA Objective 3.1b

★ ACA Objective 4.1a

★ ACA Objective 4.1b

▶ Video 5.4 Adding the Bridge Details and Strings

Drawing the Bridge and Strings of the Guitar

We must add some finishing details to the guitar to make it complete. These include the bridge details and the strings. It's possible to draw all of them using basic shapes in Illustrator.

1 Hide the Guitar Neck and Guitar Body layers in the Layers panel to reveal the placed reference image.

2 Using the Line tool, drag across the white saddle on the bridge of the guitar to create a path.

3 In the Stroke panel, set the weight of the stroke to 6pt and change the cap to Round. Select the 10% black swatch in the Swatches panel for the stroke (**Figure 5.9**).

4 Double-click the <Line> object in the Layers panel and name it **Saddle**.

Figure 5.9 Drawing a path with the Line tool and changing its properties in the Stroke panel

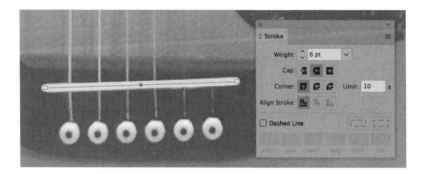

Drawing the String Pegs and Bridge

The string pegs are the part of the guitar that anchors the string into the bridge. You probably now know more about the parts of a guitar than you wanted to, but we want to accurately represent the appearance of the guitar, and the string pegs are an important part! The thing I want to stress with these elements is that there are six of them, and they all look exactly the same. This is the perfect use of symbols in Illustrator; by making a symbol and placing symbol instances, should you ever decide that you want to modify the appearance of the string pegs, you can edit one and they'll all update!

1. Begin by selecting the Ellipse tool. Draw a circle on top of one of the pegs by dragging while holding down the Shift key. Set the fill color of the circle to 10% black.

2. With the circle selected, select the Scale tool. Hold down Option (macOS) or Alt (Windows) and Shift and then start dragging above and to the left of the circle toward the center of the circle. Holding Shift scales the circle proportionally, and holding Option or Alt makes a copy, all at the same time. Release the mouse when the size is the same as the small circle of the string peg. Set the fill color to 90% black.

3. Select both circles using the Selection tool and drag them to the Symbols panel. In the Symbol Options dialog box, give the symbol a name and leave the other settings at their defaults. This creates a new symbol and the circles change to a symbol instance.

4. Using the Selection tool, hold down the Option key (macOS) or the Alt key (Windows) and drag to the position of the second string peg to make a copy of the symbol instance.

5. Press Command+D (macOS) or Ctrl+D (Windows) four times to repeat the transformation and create four more copies of the symbol instances for the other string pegs (**Figure 5.10**).

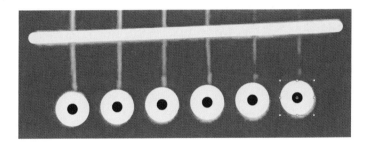

Figure 5.10 Duplicating the symbol instance of the string peg

The bridge of the guitar is a unique shape. There's certainly no tool in Illustrator that will draw that shape; however, we can begin by drawing a basic shape and then, with a few modifications, end up with the shape that we need.

1 Using the Rectangle tool, drag to draw a rectangle around the square portion of the bridge in the guitar reference image. Set the fill color to 90% black. Don't worry if it isn't exactly matching the reference image.

2 Using the Pen tool, click once at the bottom left of the rectangle where the bridge in the reference image starts to curve down, and click once at the right of the rectangle where the bridge in the reference image starts to curve down. Click one more time in the middle at the bottom of the rectangle. Doing this adds anchor points at each location that you click (**Figure 5.11**).

Figure 5.11 Adding anchor points to the rectangular shape that will become the bridge of the guitar

3 Hold down Command (macOS) or Ctrl (Windows) and drag the middle-bottom anchor point down to match the bottom of the guitar bridge in the reference image. The anchor point becomes a corner point.

4 Hold down Option (macOS) or Alt (Windows) and drag to the left on the bottom-middle anchor point to convert the corner point to a smooth point and bend the line segment (now a smooth curve) to approximately match the shape of the bridge in the reference image (**Figure 5.12**).

Figure 5.12 Changing the corner point to a smooth point to round the line segment to match the shape of the bridge

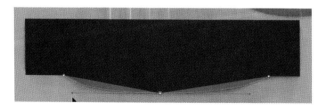

5 Adjust the stacking order of the objects in the Layers panel so that the saddle and string pegs are stacked above the bridge shape.

Drawing the Strings

At the top of the stacking order of objects for the guitar are the strings for the guitar. Because the neck of the guitar tapers at the top, we can't simply draw perfectly vertical lines for the strings. Although there are a few methods that we can use, the Pen tool makes the process easy because you don't have to drag in one long continuous motion but instead can click where the string should start, and then click where the string should end to create a path for the strings.

1 Make all of the layers of the guitar visible so you can see all of the elements that you've drawn.

2 Zoom in on the top of the neck of the guitar so you can see where the strings begin and click the Guitar layer in the Layers panel to make it the active layer.

3 Using the Pen tool, click the leftmost string to create an anchor point where the path will begin.

4 Zoom out and then zoom back in on the string pegs at the bottom of the guitar. Click in the middle of the leftmost string peg to end the path at that location.

5 Press the Escape key to terminate the drawing of the path and set the stroke width to 2 pt and the stroke color to 10% black.

6 Repeat steps 2 through 5 for the other five strings of the guitar.

7 Move the string pegs above the strings in the stacking order to create a realistic representation of the guitar (**Figure 5.13**).

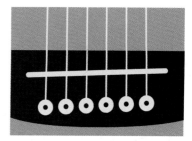

Figure 5.13 Adding the strings to the guitar and moving them below the string pegs in the stacking order

Creating and Applying a Brush

Illustrator provides several brush types that can be used to apply artwork to a path. Brushes are very powerful and make it easy to create elements that would otherwise be very time consuming to create. Illustrator contains the following brush types:

- **Calligraphic Brush:** Creates strokes that resemble those drawn with the angled point of a calligraphic pen.

- **Scatter Brush:** Disperses copies of an object (such as a flower or a star) along a path.

- **Art Brush:** Stretches artwork (such as a pencil or banner) or any other shape evenly along the length of the path.

★ *ACA Objective 4.1a*

★ *ACA Objective 2.6*

▶ *Video 5.5 Loading, Creating, and Applying Brushes*

- **Bristle Brush:** Creates brush strokes with the appearance of a natural brush with bristles.

- **Pattern Brush:** Uses individual tiles that repeat along the path. Pattern brushes can include up to five tiles, for the sides, inner corner, outer corner, beginning, and end of the pattern.

Creating the Artwork for the Brush

For most of the brush types (with the exception of calligraphic and bristle brushes), you need to first create the artwork that you want the brush to be based on. So we'll start by creating the artwork that we'll use for the design around the sound hole of the guitar.

Figure 5.14 Drawing a vertical line and an ellipse that will serve as the foundation for the brush

1 On the artboard to the right of the guitar, use the Line tool to draw a short vertical line. Select a brown stroke color and a weight of 5 pt.

2 To the side of the vertical line, use the Ellipse tool to draw a perfect circle roughly 25% of the height of the vertical line. Fill the circle with the same brown color as the line drawn in step 1 (**Figure 5.14**).

3 Select the circle using the Selection tool; then with the Pen tool, Option-click (macOS) or Alt-click (Windows) the anchor points at the top and bottom of the ellipse to convert those anchor points to corner points.

4 Select the Selection tool, grab one of the side handles of the bounding box, and reduce the width of the object to make it more of a leaf shape, as shown in **Figure 5.15**.

Figure 5.15 Reducing the width of the shape

These are the basic elements of the brush artwork that we need to create. Now we'll fine-tune the artwork so that we can create a brush from it.

1 With the leaf shape selected using the Selection tool, hover over one of the corners of the bounding box until you see a rotation icon. Drag to rotate the shape about 45 degrees.

2 Using the Reflect tool ▣, click once on the line. Hold down Option and Shift (macOS) or Alt and Shift (Windows), and click further down on the line to reflect the selected shape across the vertical axis of the line (**Figure 5.16**).

3 Using the Selection tool, select all three shapes, and then click again on any of the three shapes to define it as the key object.

4 Open the Align panel by choosing Window > Align. From the Align panel menu, choose Show Options. In the Distribute Spacing section at the

Figure 5.16 Reflecting the shape across the vertical axis of the line

bottom of the panel, make sure that the value in the field is 0; then click the Horizontal Distribute Space ⊞ button to remove the space between the selected objects.

5 Duplicate the two leaf shapes vertically along the line and change the color of the alternating leaves to shades of the original brown color (**Figure 5.17**). Send the shapes behind the vertical line.

Figure 5.17 Changing the colors of the alternating leaves

Creating the Brush

With the artwork created, we'll use that as the basis for a brush. We'll then apply that brush to a path around the outside of the sound hole.

1 Reduce the length of the line so that it aligns with the top of the leaf shapes and protrudes slightly below the leaf shapes at the bottom.

2 Select all of the shapes in the artwork and rotate them 90 degrees clockwise.

3 Open the Brushes panel by choosing Window > Brushes and drag the artwork onto the Brushes panel. The New Brush dialog box appears.

4 Select Pattern Brush and click OK.

   A pattern brush uses the artwork used to create the brush and repeats it, as a tile, along a path. As you can see in the Pattern Brush Options dialog box, you can define unique patterns for the start and end as well as the outside and inside corners of a path. Because we're applying this brush to a circle, we don't have to worry about anything except the side tile. If you were applying this brush to any shape that contained corners, you'd want to take care and create an appropriate tile for the inside and outside corners as well.

5 Enter **Inlay** in the name field and change all of the tile options except the side tile to None (**Figure 5.18**). Click OK.

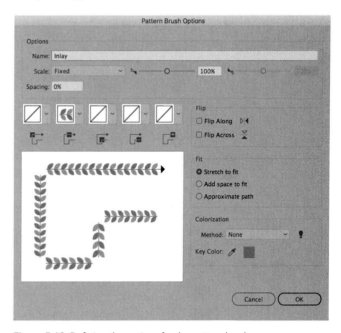

Figure 5.18 Defining the options for the pattern brush

6 Once the brush is created, you can delete the artwork that you used to create the brush by selecting it and pressing Delete or Backspace.

Applying the Brush

A brush can be used by drawing with the Paintbrush tool ![paintbrush icon] or it can be applied to an existing path. The method you choose will depend on the artwork you're creating and how you prefer to create it.

1 Using the Selection tool, select the sound hole of the guitar.

2 Select the Scale tool, position the mouse pointer outside the sound hole (but between the anchor points on the circle), and press Option and Shift (macOS) or Alt and Shift (Windows). Then drag away from the center of the shape. (Holding Option or Alt duplicates the shape, and holding Shift enlarges the duplicate proportionally.) When the circle is about half an inch larger than the original sound hole, release the mouse button.

3 Set the fill and stroke color of the shape to None; then in the Brushes panel, click the brush that you just created to apply the brush to the selected path.

Initially, the brush will most likely be bigger than desired. The beauty of brushes, however, is that you can dynamically adjust the size of the brush by changing the stroke weight of the path.

4 Adjust the stroke weight until the inlay appears at a size that you prefer.

Editing a Brush

It's bound to happen. You create a brush and then later realize that you want to edit some element of the brush such as the shape or color. Illustrator makes this process easy. Call it a bug or call it a feature, but when you have a template layer in your document, it can inhibit the ability to edit a brush. So before you proceed, turn off the visibility of the template layer in the document.

1 Open the Brushes panel by choosing Window > Brushes.

2 Drag the Inlay brush from the Brushes panel onto the artboard. The artwork that makes up the brush will now appear on the artboard.

3 The artwork will be grouped by default, so with the artwork selected, choose Object > Ungroup (you may need to do this twice to release all the groups).

4 Edit the artwork as desired; then select all the artwork, and while holding down Option (macOS) or Alt (Window), drag the artwork on top of the existing brush in the Brushes panel to replace the brush with your new artwork. When the Pattern Brush Options dialog box appears, click OK.

5   You'll be presented with a dialog box asking you if you'd like to apply the new brush appearance to existing strokes that have the brush applied or if you'd like to leave the strokes with the old appearance. Choose Apply To Strokes to apply the new brush to the inlay of the guitar (**Figure 5.19**).

Figure 5.19 The brush applied to the inlay around the sound hole

Using Image Trace to Create Distressed Text

Now that the guitar has been created for the poster, we need some background elements to fill the poster. We'll use text elements using various fonts, sizes, and shapes to populate the background of the poster. We don't want plain-old text, though. It would be nice to have distressed text to give more visual interest to the design, and to do that, we'll have Illustrator trace some photos to convert them to vector graphics. We can then use them to provide that distressed look to the text.

★ ACA Objective 4.5d

★ ACA Objective 2.4b

★ ACA Objective 3.2b

★ ACA Objective 4.3c

▶ **Video 5.6** *Running Image Trace on an Image*

Running Image Trace

Sometimes the raster image you need to convert to a vector image is more complex than our guitar body. Tracing it by hand with the Pen tools or any of the other drawing tools available in Illustrator may be impossible (or at the very least, impractical). That's where Image Trace comes to the rescue! This very powerful Illustrator feature does a great job of tracing raster images automatically—and gives you a lot of control over the quality of the output.

1 Create a new layer in the Layers panel at the top of the stacking order called **Text Background**. This is where we'll put the text elements for the background of the design.

2 Choose File > Place. In the dialog box that appears, navigate to the exercise files that were included with this course, select the **Wood.jpg** file, and click Place or OK.

3 Your cursor will change to the loaded graphics pointer. Clicking once will place the image at 100%. That's too big for what we need, so instead, drag to scale the image roughly to the empty area to the right of the guitar. This places the image in the document (**Figure 5.20**).

Figure 5.20 Placing and sizing the wood image

Next we'll convert the placed image into a vector element using the Image Trace feature.

1 With the image selected, click the Image Trace button in the Control or Properties panel. Illustrator runs Image Trace on the image using the default preset.

2   Feel free to choose different options from the Preset menu in the Control or Properties panel to see how each preset produces a different result. When you're finished, choose the Default preset and click the Image Trace Panel button ▦ in the Control or Properties panel to display the Image Trace panel.

3   In the Image Trace panel, click the disclosure triangle next to Advanced to display more options. Select Ignore White to instruct Illustrator to make the white areas transparent.

It's worth noting that each time you make an adjustment to the options in the Image Trace panel, Illustrator has to reprocess the image. The higher the resolution of the image, the longer this can take.

4   At this point, the image is a special Image Trace object, not editable paths. To convert the object to editable paths (**Figure 5.21**), click Expand in the Control or Properties panel. Close the Image Trace panel.

Keep in mind that you can use any image you wish for this effect. Patterns give amazing results and can be used for many design elements. In this example, we're using one to create a distressed look in the text, but you can use patterns for a background or anything else as well. When I'm out and about, I use my phone to take pictures of all kinds of patterns that I could eventually use in a future design.

Figure 5.21 Expanding the image trace object to editable paths

Distressing the Type

We'll use the Image Trace pattern that we created earlier to distress some text that we'll place in the document.

1   Using the Type tool, add some text to the document. The word JAZZ was used in the example shown, but you can type anything you want. Use any font you wish and size and kern the type to taste.

We're going to use the type as a mask; to do this, we'll convert the type to outlines so we can use the Type as a shape. Whenever you do this, you might want to make a copy of the live text before you convert it to outlines in case you need to make an edit to the text later.

2   With the text selected, choose Type > Create Outlines.

The purpose of the next steps is to end up with one complete compound path instead of several individual ones. Illustrator doesn't know how you intend to use the outlined text, so you need to simplify the shape in order to use it as a clipping mask later.

3   Choose Object > Ungroup to ungroup the elements.

4   Choose Object > Compound Path > Release to release the compound paths.

5   Choose Object > Compound Path > Make.

6   Create a copy of the wood pattern so you can use it for other text elements that you'll be creating and position the wood pattern behind the outlined text the way you'd like it to appear within the mask. (I rotated mine 90° clockwise so the grain parallels the text.) Select both the text and the wood shape using the Selection tool, and choose Object > Clipping Mask > Make. The outlined text now masks the wood pattern, creating distressed text (**Figure 5.22**).

Figure 5.22 Selecting the outlined text and the wood pattern (left). The resulting clipping mask (right).

7 Double-click the text with the Selection tool to enter isolation mode, and select the wood pattern. Apply a different fill color to change the appearance of the distressed text.

8 Repeat steps 1 through 4 to create other text elements to fill most of the background of the poster.

Using Envelope Distort to Distort Text to a Specific Shape

★ ACA Objective 4.4b

★ ACA Objective 4.5b

It's fairly easy to fill in the background of the poster using text objects, but it gets a bit tricky around the curved shape of the guitar. For this, we'll use a technique for distorting objects into any form we wish, allowing us to create uniquely shaped elements in our design (**Figure 5.23**).

▶ Video 5.7
Distorting Objects Using the Envelope Distort Feature

1 Start by creating some text that you'd like to use to fill in an area.

2 In the Layers panel, unlock the Guitar layer. In the document, select the guitar body; notice that a small colored square appears at the far right of the Guitar layer listing on the Layers panel (in the *selection column*). Make a copy of the guitar body by Option-dragging (macOS) or Alt-dragging (Windows) the colored square onto the Text Background layer. Lock the Guitar layer again.

3 With the copy of the guitar body selected, choose Object > Path > Offset Path. Enter a value of **.25 in** in the Offset field and click OK. This setting offsets the path from its original location by .25 in. This creates a copy of the guitar body, so delete the original guitar body shape that you started with.

4 Using the Rectangle tool, draw one rectangle in each area where you'd like the text to appear. Make sure the rectangles overlap the body of the guitar.

Figure 5.23 The poster showing gaps that need to be filled

Figure 5.24 Removing areas of the rectangles using the Shape Builder tool to create the shapes that we'll use to distort the text

Figure 5.25 The poster with the distorted text added to fill the spaces

5 Select the guitar body and the two rectangle shapes using the Selection tool. Now with the Shape Builder tool, Option-click (macOS) or Alt-click (Windows) the guitar body shape and the areas where the rectangles overlap the guitar body to remove those elements (**Figure 5.24**).

Using Envelope Distort

The objective of the previous steps is to create shapes that we'll be using to distort the text. The two remaining shapes represent the empty areas of the text background that we want to fill.

1 Using the Type tool, create some text that you'd like to use to fill the two areas of the poster. You don't need to size these text objects precisely, because the Envelope Distort filter will do most of the work for you.

2 Select both shapes and choose Object > Arrange > Bring To Front. The shapes that you'll use to distort the text need to be above the text objects in the stacking order.

3 Select the first shape and the text using the Selection tool and choose Object > Envelope Distort > Make With Top Object. The text is morphed to match the shape that was selected and above the text in the stacking order.

   If you look in the Layers panel, you'll notice that the object you just created is a unique envelope object. To create the distressed text, we need to expand this into a basic compound path.

4 With the distorted text object selected, choose Object > Expand. In the Expand dialog box that appears, select both Object and Fill, and click OK. Choose Object > Ungroup twice; then choose Object > Compound Path > Release. Finally, choose Object > Compound Path > Make to create one complete compound path.

5 Add the texture to this shape using the techniques learned earlier in this chapter. Repeat steps 1 through 4 for the remaining area of the poster (**Figure 5.25**).

Adding Effects to the Music Poster

★ ACA Objective 4.6a

★ ACA Objective 3.1b

★ ACA Objective 3.2a

▶ **Video 5.8** *Adding Effects to the Music Poster*

The text background of the poster looks great, but on the white background the text elements are getting lost and are hard to see clearly. In this section, we'll add a colored background to the poster and then add some Adobe Photoshop effects to both the text elements and the background to make it easier to see the text. Photoshop effects created in Illustrator are pixel-based effects but are still editable easily within Illustrator.

1. Begin by creating a new layer in the Layers panel and name that layer **Background**. Move the layer below the Guitar layer in the layer stacking order.

2. On the Background layer, use the Rectangle tool to draw a rectangle to the bleed guides in the document. Fill the rectangle with a color of your choice. I used C:55, M:31, Y:100, and K:13, but feel free to use whatever color looks good with your design.

3. With the Rectangle selected, open the Effect menu and in the Photoshop Effects section, choose Effect Gallery. In the dialog box that appears, you'll see a listing of all the Photoshop (raster-based) effects that can be applied to the selected shape.

4. Open the Texture category in the options displayed to the right of the dialog box and select Texturizer. From the Texture menu, choose Canvas and set Scaling to 85, Relief to 8, and Light to Top (**Figure 5.26**). Feel free to experiment with these settings until you have a texture that you like. Click OK.

5. Lock the Background layer to prevent further editing of the layer.

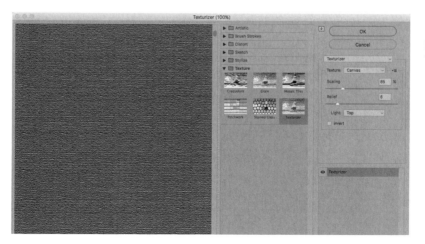

Figure 5.26 Adding a Photoshop effect to the background rectangle in the poster

Adding Effects to the Text Background Layer

To give the text on the Text Background layer more depth and to make the text stand out a bit more, we'll add a drop shadow effect to the entire layer. The benefit of targeting the layer and applying an effect to it is that everything on the layer will contain that same effect, and anything new added to that layer will automatically have that effect applied as well.

1. Make all of the layers visible except for the Template layer and lock all of the layers except for the Text Background layer.

2. Click the target circle ⭘ to the right of the Text Background layer in the Layers panel. This targets the entire layer.

3. Open the Effect menu and in the Illustrator Effects section, choose Stylize > Drop Shadow to open the Drop Shadow dialog box. Adjust the X and Y Offset values to set the size of the drop shadow and change the Blur value to set the softness of the drop shadow. Use the values you prefer and adjust the color if desired (**Figure 5.27**). Click OK.

    Notice that the target circle is now filled in ◎, which indicates that the layer is targeted and it has appearance attributes applied to it.

As you can see in **Figure 5.28**, adding a colored background, applying a texture with lighting effects, and applying a drop shadow to our text really gave our poster some depth and made the graphics pop!

Figure 5.27 ▲ Applying a drop shadow to the Text Background layer

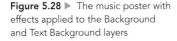

Figure 5.28 ▶ The music poster with effects applied to the Background and Text Background layers

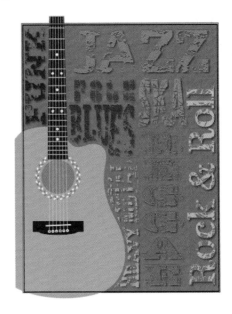

Placing Text and Linking Text Areas

★ ACA Objective 4.2

Our music poster is looking great, but there's no information on the poster telling the audience what the event is and when it's taking place. We'll add some text to the poster to provide this information.

▶ **Video 5.9** Placing Text from an External File

1   Zoom in on the bottom of the guitar body. Create a new layer called **Text** and lock the other layers in the Layers panel.

2   Using the Type tool, create a point type or area type object (you choose) and enter a title for the music festival and a date on a second line. See **Figure 5.29** for reference, but feel free to enter your own event name and date.

3   Choose File > Place to open the Place dialog box, select the `2018 Bands.txt` file, and click Place. In the Text Import Options dialog box, leave the settings at their defaults and click OK.

Figure 5.29 Adding a title and date to the music poster

4   Your cursor changes to the loaded graphics pointer, which indicates that Illustrator is ready to place the text in the document. Drag to create a text area roughly half the width of the title text. All of the text from the text file is placed in the text area that you've drawn.

5   Select all of the text in the text area with your Type tool, increase the point size, and change the font as well as the color of the text. You'll likely see a + sign in the lower-right corner of the area type object. This + sign indicates overset text, which means there's more text in the area type object than can currently be displayed.

Figure 5.30 Flowing the text between two area type objects

6   Using the Selection tool, click the + sign and your cursor changes to the loaded graphics pointer again. Drag out a second area type object to the right of the first and to link the two type areas together. You'll notice a link indicator connecting the two frames and the overset text flows into the newly created type area (**Figure 5.30**). Using the Selection tool, adjust the size of the area type objects by dragging their handles.

★ ACA Objective 4.2e

Packaging the Project

▶ **Video 5.10**
*Packaging the
Elements of
the Project for
Distribution*

Whenever you want to send an Illustrator file to another user, whether it is another designer to add some elements to a project or a service provider or printer to output/print the project, you need to include all the dependencies required by the file. These dependencies include any linked graphics or fonts used in the project. You see, Illustrator wants to ensure that the project looks the same regardless of who opens it or on what computer it's opened. To ensure that the recipient has all the elements needed, we'll perform a package operation in Illustrator that includes all linked graphics and fonts required to work on the file.

1 Save the most recent changes to your work by choosing File > Save.

2 Choose File > Package to initiate the package operation and to display the Package dialog box. Choose a location for the package folder that Illustrator will create, and be sure to provide a relevant name for it in the Folder Name field (**Figure 5.31**).

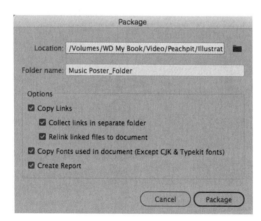

Figure 5.31 Packaging the Illustrator file

The Options section of the Package dialog box lets you determine what is included in the package and how the files get packaged. The options available are as follows:

- **Copy Links:** Any placed images that are linked in the Illustrator file will be copied to the package folder.

- **Collect Links In A Separate Folder:** All copied links will be organized into a separate Links folder as a subfolder of the package folder.

- **Relink Linked Files To Document:** The folder paths to the linked items that were placed in the Illustrator file will be updated to point to the linked items in the package folder.

- **Copy Fonts Used In Document (Except CJK & Typekit Fonts):** All fonts used in the Illustrator file will be copied to the package folder except for Chinese, Japanese, and Korean fonts as well as Typekit fonts. Provided recipients are Creative Cloud subscribers, they can activate these fonts easily on their own system.

- **Create Report:** Generates a summary of the packaged elements as a text file.

3 Click the Package button to package all the elements of the file to a new folder. You'll be presented with a warning message making you aware of the legal ramifications of sharing fonts with other users. Check with the vendor(s) of the font(s) that you are using to ensure you're being compliant when sharing fonts with other users. Click OK.

4 When the package process is complete, you'll be presented with a window indicating that the packaging process is complete, along with options to dismiss the window or to show the location of the package folder in the Finder (macOS) or the Windows Explorer (Windows) (**Figure 5.32**).

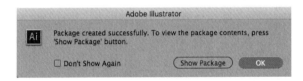

Figure 5.32 The window that appears when the package operation is complete

Congratulations! You've completed the music event poster! This chapter covered a lot of ground, and ideally you learned a lot of new techniques that you can use when building your own projects.

CHAPTER OBJECTIVES

Chapter Learning Objectives

- Place photos into an Adobe Illustrator file.
- Use the Shape Builder tool to create artwork.
- Work with text in Illustrator.
- Understand color mode settings for web documents.
- Save files for web use.
- Use Export For Web and Export For Screens.

Chapter ACA Objectives

For full descriptions of the objectives, see the table on pages 196–204.

DOMAIN 2.0
PROJECT SETUP AND INTERFACE
2.1a, 2.4

DOMAIN 3.0
ORGANIZATION OF DOCUMENTS
3.1

DOMAIN 4.0
CREATE AND MODIFY VISUAL ELEMENTS
4.1, 4.1a, 4.2, 4.4, 4.5b, 4.6c

DOMAIN 5.0
PUBLISHING DIGITAL MEDIA
5.1a, 5.2, 5.2b

CHAPTER 6

Creating and Exporting Content for Web and Mobile Projects

In this chapter you'll create a mockup for a mobile application. Adobe Illustrator CC offers several advantages for this type of work, namely the fact that by using vector content you can easily make adjustments to elements without loss of quality. In addition, Illustrator gives us several tools that we can use for exporting that vector-based content to web graphics for use during web development.

Creating a Document for a Mobile Device

We'll begin by creating a new document in Illustrator at the size of a mobile device. Illustrator offers several presets in the Mobile category when you are creating a new document. If you don't see the mobile device size that you're looking for, you can enter custom values in the Width and Height fields in the New Document dialog box.

1 With Illustrator open on your computer, choose File > New or click the Create New button in the Start workspace to open the New Document dialog box.

★ ACA Objective 2.1a
★ ACA Objective 5.1a
★ ACA Objective 5.2b

▶ **Video 6.1** *Creating an Illustrator File at the Size of a Mobile Screen*

2   Click the Mobile category at the top of the dialog box to view all presets based on the Mobile profile, and select the iPhone 6 Plus preset. Click the Create button and save the document as **Mobile Mockup.ai** (**Figure 6.1**).

Because you're creating a document based on a Mobile preset, the units of measurement are set to pixels, the color mode is set to RGB, and the Raster Effects resolution is set to 72 ppi.

3   Open the Layers panel. Double-click Layer 1 and rename it **Interface**.

4   Make sure the Align Art To Pixel Grid button  is selected in the Control panel; then select the Rectangle tool and click anywhere on the artboard. In the Rectangle dialog box, enter **1242 px** and **200 px** in the Width and Height fields, respectively. Click OK.

5   Set the fill color of the Rectangle to black and the stroke to None. Move the rectangle to the top of the artboard and align it to the top and sides.

6   Using the Selection tool, hold down Option (macOS) or Alt (Windows) and drag a copy of the rectangle to the bottom of the artboard (**Figure 6.2**).

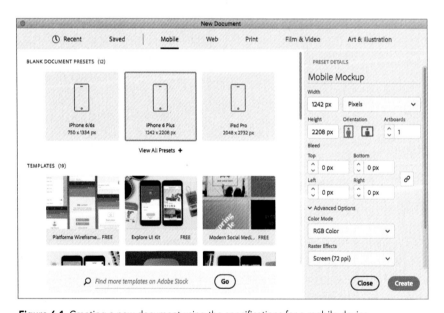

Figure 6.1 Creating a new document using the specifications for a mobile device

Figure 6.2 Setting up the interface of the mobile design

Creating the Icons for the Mobile Mockup

★ ACA Objective 4.1a

★ ACA Objective 4.4

★ ACA Objective 4.5b

★ ACA Objective 4.6c

As you're well aware by now, the major strength of Adobe Illustrator is drawing vector artwork. Icons most definitely fall into this category. In this chapter, you'll see how Illustrator makes this process relatively easy. Beginning with some basic shapes, we'll create some useful icons for this project.

▶ **Video 6.2** *Creating the Icons for the Mobile Mockup*

Creating the Hamburger Icon for the Mobile Mockup

The mockup for our mobile application uses a few unique icons that we need to create for the design of this piece. It's useful to know that you can also download existing art by selecting a template in the New Document dialog box or by downloading artwork from *stock.adobe.com* (purchase required for access to stock photos and artwork).

1   Open the Layers panel.

2   Create a new layer called **Icons** on which you'll be drawing the icons for the mobile mockup.

3   Using the Line tool, drag to draw a short horizontal line about 150 px long in the upper-left corner of the mobile interface. In the Stroke panel, set the stroke weight to 20 px and select Round for the cap. In the Color panel, set the stroke color to 156 Red, 193 Green, and 0 Blue.

As stated before, it's a good idea to add this color to your Swatches panel and set that swatch to be a global color. That way, it's easy to reuse the color later, and if you should decide that you want a different color, you can edit the swatch and every object with that swatch applied to it will update instantly.

4   Using the Selection tool, Option-drag (macOS) or Alt-drag (Windows) the line to make a copy. While dragging, add the Shift key to keep the copy of the line aligned with the original line. Release the mouse to create the aligned copy.

5   Press Command+D (macOS) or Ctrl+D (Windows) to repeat the last transformation so that you have a total of three lines stacked on top of one another, creating the hamburger icon (**Figure 6.3**).

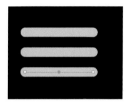

Figure 6.3 Drawing the hamburger icon for the mockup

Drawing the Icons at the Bottom of the Mockup

Like most mobile applications, ours uses a row of unique icons at the bottom of the interface. Let's draw those icons now.

DRAWING THE FAVORITES ICON

1 Using the Star tool, click once on the artboard to display the Star dialog box. Enter **80 px** for Radius 1, **40 px** for Radius 2, and **5** for Points. Click OK to create the Star.

2 Position the star on top of the black rectangle at the bottom of the interface, set the fill color to the green color swatch that you created earlier in the chapter, and set the stroke color to None.

DRAWING THE LOCATION ICON

1 Using the Ellipse tool, draw a circle that is about 75 px in diameter. Fill this shape with the green swatch.

2 Switch to the Pen tool and Option-click (macOS) or Alt-click (Windows) on the bottom anchor point of the shape to convert the smooth anchor point to a corner point.

3 Hold down Command (macOS) or Ctrl (Windows) to temporarily access the Direct Selection tool. Drag the bottom anchor point down until this icon is the same size as the star shape (**Figure 6.4**).

4 Draw a smaller circle on top of this shape and position it in the center but toward the top of the larger shape.

5 Select both of the shapes and choose Object > Compound Path > Make.

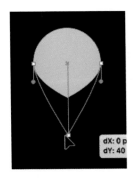

Figure 6.4 Dragging the anchor point down to reshape the object

DRAWING THE HEART

This technique is a great example of achieving the desired result using a method that you might not expect would produce that result.

1 Using the Rectangle tool, draw a square and then rotate the square shape 45 degrees.

2 Draw another rectangle that overlaps the square covering the top but revealing a triangle shape at the bottom.

3 Select both shapes; then select the Shape Builder tool. Hold down Option (macOS) or Alt (Windows) and click the top two shapes, leaving only the triangle shape remaining at the bottom (**Figure 6.5**).

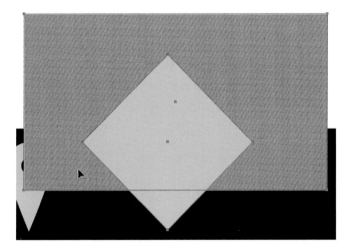

Figure 6.5 Using the Shape Builder tool to produce a small triangle

4 Using the Direct Selection tool, click the top line segment of the triangle to select it, and then press Delete or Backspace to delete the top line segment, leaving an open path that is still the same shape.

5 Set the stroke color to the green swatch we saved earlier and the fill color to None. In the Stroke panel, set the cap to round and increase the stroke weight until the triangle looks like a heart shape.

6 Choose Object > Expand. Select Fill and Stroke and click OK. Scale the heart shape to the desired size.

DRAWING THE ADD ICON

We don't have to reinvent the wheel to draw this icon. As a matter of fact, if you wanted to, you could grab the Type tool, type a + character, pick a font that you like, and just convert it to outlines. There's no wrong way to do this! Explore, enjoy, be creative! We'll take a more primitive approach and draw the Add icon using some basic shapes.

1 Using the Rectangle tool, draw a rectangle that is tall and skinny but the height of the other icons at the bottom of the interface.

2 With the rectangle selected, choose Edit > Copy, and then Edit > Paste In Front to put a duplicate copy right on top of the first one.

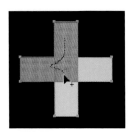

Figure 6.6 Using the Shape Builder tool to merge the two rectangles together

3 Rotate the copy of the rectangle 90 degrees based on the center of the shape.

4 Select both rectangles and drag across the shapes using the Shape Builder tool to merge the two shapes into one (**Figure 6.6**).

DRAWING THE INFO ICON

The last icon we have to draw is the Info icon. You see this in a lot of apps; it's the icon that people tap when they want to know more information.

1 Using the Ellipse tool, draw a perfect circle that is the height of the other icons. Fill this circle with the green color as well.

2 Using the Type tool, click once on the artboard to create a point type object and type the letter **i**. Adjust the font and size of the i so that it fits within the circle.

3 Select the i character using the Selection tool and choose Type > Create Outlines.

4 Position and size the i character inside the circle. Select the character and the circle, and then choose Object > Compound Path > Make. This punches the i character through the circle shape (**Figure 6.7**).

Figure 6.7 Creating a compound path for the Info icon

5 Distribute the space between the icons at the bottom of the document by positioning the left- and rightmost icons where you want them. Then select all of the icons and click the Horizontal Distribute Space icon at the bottom of the Align panel.

THE PATHFINDER PANEL

Although this chapter and the accompanying videos use the Shape Builder tool to create new shapes from existing shapes, the tried-and-true Pathfinder panel can also be used to achieve the same result. At the top of the Pathfinder panel, you'll find buttons that activate four different shape modes, each of which performs a different action based on the stacking order of the selected objects (**Figure 6.8**). The stacking order of the objects is very important when using the Pathfinder panel, so if you don't get the result you're expecting, oftentimes adjusting the stacking order will address the problem.

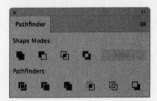

Figure 6.8 The Pathfinder panel

The Shape Mode buttons in the top row of the Pathfinder panel are

- **Unite:** Combines the selected objects into an object
- **Minus Front:** Removes the overlapping objects from the bottom shape
- **Intersect:** Removes everything except where all of the selected overlapping objects intersect
- **Exclude:** Similar to Intersect except the overlapping area of two objects is removed, leaving everything else intact

In our mockup, you could have used Unite to make the plus icon, and Minus Front to create the Heart and Info icons.

It's worth noting that you can also use these shape modes to produce editable effects by holding down Option (macOS) or Alt (Windows) while clicking a shape mode button. Shapes created this way are called compound shapes.

Not to be overlooked, the bottom row of buttons in the Pathfinder panel allow you to apply Pathfinder operations as effects. Pathfinder effects can be applied to any combination of objects, groups, or layers.

Pathfinder operations can also be applied from the Effect > Pathfinder menu but can be used only on groups, layers, and text objects. See the Illustrator User Guide at *https://helpx.adobe.com/illustrator/user-guide.html* for more information.

★ ACA Objective 3.1

★ ACA Objective 2.4

★ ACA Objective 4.2

▶ **Video 6.3** *Adding Text and Images to the Mobile Mockup*

Adding Text and Photos

In this section, we'll add the finishing touches to the project by adding some text and photographic elements to represent the appearance of the app in its final form.

1   In the Layers panel, create a new layer called **Photo Elements**. This is where you'll put the imagery for the design.

2   Choose File > Place and navigate to your exercise files folder and select the file called `Butterfly.psd`. Make sure that Link is selected, and then click Place. Position the subject of the photo in the main area of the app between the top and bottom rectangles in the document.

3   Temporarily hide the photo, and using the Rectangle tool, draw a rectangle in the main area of the artboard between the rectangles located at the top and bottom of the page.

4   Make the photo visible, and using the Selection tool, select the photo and the rectangle and choose Object > Clipping Mask > Make. You've made a clipping mask that clips the placed image to the bounds of the rectangle (**Figure 6.9**).

Figure 6.9 Placing the `Butterfly.psd` photo in position on the mockup and cropping it with a clipping mask

Creating the Divisions of the Main Screen

On the main screen of the mobile site, there will be three sections that a user can tap to navigate to a particular area of the site. In this section we'll create those sections by simulating the appearance of the main screen being divided into three different areas.

1   Using the Rectangle tool, drag out another rectangle the size of the main screen. This should be the exact same size as the previous rectangle that you drew.

2   With the rectangle selected, open the Transform panel and deselect the Constrain Width And Height Proportions icon so you can adjust the width and height of the object independently. Now click one of the top points of the Reference point icon ▦ and in the height (H) field, type /3 after the current value. This sets the height of the rectangle to 1/3 of the original height.

3   Hold down Option (macOS) or Alt (Windows) and drag to create a copy of the rectangle below the current one. Be sure to align the top of the copy to the bottom of the original rectangle. Fill the rectangle with black.

4   Make another copy of the rectangle and position it below the second rectangle to create a third rectangle. Fill this one with black as well.

5   Select the second rectangle and open the Transparency panel. Set the blending mode to Color and Opacity to 70%. This gives the second section a desaturated look yet still with some color to the photo.

6   Finally, select the third rectangle, and in the Transparency panel, change the blend mode to Color with an Opacity value of 100%. This completely desaturates the image, giving it a black and white appearance (**Figure 6.10**).

Adding Text to the Mobile Mockup

We're almost finished with the design; we just need to add some text for the title of the mobile design and then some additional text for the individual sections of the design.

1   Using the Type tool, click to create a point type object and type the text **The Insectarium**. Change the font to one of your choosing and adjust the size to fit in the rectangle at the top of the screen. We used Clavo Medium at 107 pt. Change the text color to white.

2   Using the Rectangle tool, drag to draw a thin rectangle that is as wide as the artboard and about 120 px tall. Move this rectangle to the bottom of the first section and set the fill color of the rectangle to black and the opacity to 50%.

3   Using the Type tool, add some point type with the text **Butterflies** and set the color to white and adjust the font and size to fit within the rectangle. Align the text visually within the rectangle.

4   Select the text and the rectangle and duplicate them to the second and third sections of the design. Change the text for section two to **Insects** and section three to **Other** (**Figure 6.11**).

Figure 6.10 After dividing the image area of the mobile mockup into three sections

Figure 6.11 Adding the text and rectangle to each of the three sections of the design

Creating Web Graphics Using Save For Web

▶ *Video 6.4 Saving to Web-Based Formats Using the Save For Web Command*

Now that the design of the mobile site is finished, we need to provide the web developers with image assets to use to produce the finished product. One way to do this is using the Save For Web command. This command gives users the ability to control how web assets are generated from the Illustrator artwork.

Creating Slices

Slices are a way to divide your artwork into individual sections, each of which can be formatted as an independent image and can use the format of your choosing. Although you can manually create slices using the Slice tool ✐, there are more accurate ways to get the job done that you'll learn in the following steps.

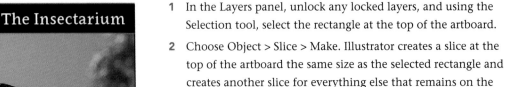

1 In the Layers panel, unlock any locked layers, and using the Selection tool, select the rectangle at the top of the artboard.

2 Choose Object > Slice > Make. Illustrator creates a slice at the top of the artboard the same size as the selected rectangle and creates another slice for everything else that remains on the artboard.

3 Select the rectangle that encompasses the first section of the main screen and choose Object > Slice > Make.

4 Repeat steps 1 through 3 for section two and three as well as the rectangle at the bottom of the artboard (**Figure 6.12**).

Figure 6.12 Creating slices for the individual elements of the design

Using Save For Web

Now that we have sliced the design, we can export those individual slices to various web formats based on the content of each slice. Web formats can be a bit confusing and misunderstood, so here's a list of the common web formats and the preferred use for each format:

- **JPEG**—The JPEG (Joint Photographic Experts Group) format is commonly used due to its ability to compress files to very small sizes. This compression is applied based on a sliding scale between quality and file size. It's important to know that the JPEG format utilizes lossy compression, which means some data is thrown away when saving to this format. How much data is discarded depends on the quality/size slider setting that is used. The JPEG format is best used for continuous tone images (photographs).

- **GIF**—The GIF (Graphics Interchange Format) format is best used for artwork that contains areas of solid color, such as text and logos (not photographs). One of the advantages of the GIF format is its ability to include transparency in the image. This is useful for removing the background color of artwork so that it can be used on any background color that you choose when placing it in a web page.

- **PNG-8**—The PNG-8 (Portable Network Graphics) format is similar to the GIF format. Both work best with images that have blocks of color (as opposed to continuous tone images) and that contain a limited number of colors ("8-bit color"). Because PNG-8 compresses files more efficiently than GIF, it's gained popularity now that browser support is widespread. Another advantage is that PNG-8 can include multilevel transparency for elements such as drop shadows.

- **PNG-24**—The PNG-24 format shares many of the advantages of PNG-8 including support for continuous tone images ("24-bit color"). It's become quite popular as a replacement for the JPEG format because it can contain multilevel transparency for elements such as drop shadows, whereas the JPEG format doesn't support transparency at all. Also, both PNG formats use lossless compression, so no data is lost with reduced file sizes.

- **SVG**—The SVG (Scalable Vector Graphics) format is the only vector format of all the formats in this list. In the advent of adaptive and responsive web design, the ability to scale vector graphics is a huge advantage for designers and developers.

There are multiple methods for exporting web image assets from Illustrator. The traditional method uses the Save For Web command. In recent versions of Illustrator, the word *legacy* has been added to this command to indicate that there's a newer feature (covered later in this chapter) that offers some advantages.

1 Choose File > Export > Save For Web (Legacy). The Save For Web dialog box opens.

2 Using the Slice tool in the Save For Web dialog box, you can click each slice to select it and then choose an export format for the selected slice in the right side of the dialog box.

You can choose the format and settings for each slice, but you can also choose a preset from the Name menu in the Preset area in the upper right of the dialog box. You can specify pixel dimensions in the Image Size area if you need a size other than what is defined on the artboard.

3   Click the slices at the top and bottom of the artboard and choose PNG-8 128 Dithered from the Name menu.

4   Click the remaining slices and choose PNG-24 from the Name menu. You can Shift-click to select multiple slices at the same time (**Figure 6.13**).

5   Click Save and choose a location in which the images will be saved. Click the second Save button to save the images.

Figure 6.13 Defining the output formats of the individual slices in the Save For Web dialog box

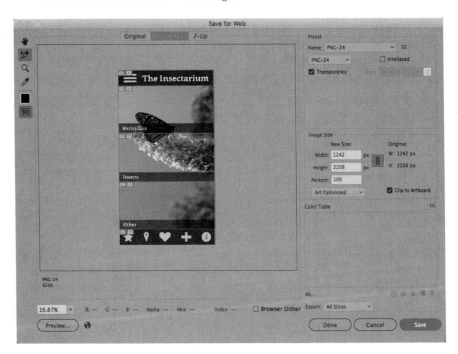

Using Export for Screens to Generate Web and Mobile Assets

★ ACA Objective 5.2

The Save For Web command works well, but if you need to export individual elements of your design, it isn't much help. Fortunately, Illustrator has the Save For Screens command, which makes it easy to get more granular with your design elements and export exactly the items that you need at the size and in the format(s) that you need them.

▶ **Video 6.5** *Using Export for Screens to Create Assets for Web and Mobile Use*

1 Choose View > Hide Slices to hide the slices that you defined in the previous section.

2 Choose File > Export > Export For Screens. In the Export For Screens dialog box (**Figure 6.14**), notice that selecting the Artboard tab at the top allows you to export each artboard in your document as an individual file.

   The section on the right side of the Export For Screens dialog box gives you the ability to choose the range of artboards you want to export as well as the location of the exported files. You can also add scale factors, which will create additional images of each artboard at the scale factor and in the format that you desire.

3 Click the Export Artboard button to export the artboard assets.

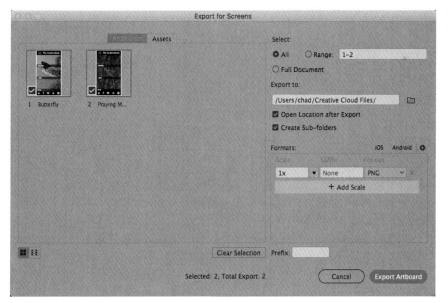

Figure 6.14 Exporting the artboards using the Export For Screens dialog box

Exporting Individual Assets

1   Choose File > Export > Export For Screens to display the Export For Screens dialog box. Click the Assets tab at the top of the dialog box; then click the Asset Export Panel button in the middle of the Assets tab.

You can also get to the Asset Export panel by choosing Window > Asset Export.

2   Select the Favorite icon at the bottom of the mockup and drag it to the Asset Export panel. The artwork is added to the panel. Click the name to highlight it and assign a more appropriate name if desired. Repeat for the remainder of the icons at the bottom of the mockup.

Figure 6.15 Assets added to the Asset Export panel

3   Select the three lines that make up the hamburger icon at the top left of the design and drag them to the Asset Export panel. Whoops! Each line got added individually to the panel. Good to know in the future, but not what we want! Choose Edit > Undo. Now, hold Option (macOS) or Alt (Windows) and drag the lines to the Asset Export panel. This time, all of the items are added as a single asset (**Figure 6.15**).

4   If desired, click the Add Scale button to add an additional size for each of the assets in the Asset Export panel. When doing so, you can define a scale factor, suffix, and format for the additional asset.

5   Choose File > Export > Export For Screens. In the Export For Screens dialog box, click the Assets tab. Each icon from the Asset Export panel is shown with the same options available for format and scaling that we saw previously. Select each asset that you wish to export or select All Assets to export all assets.

6   Click the Export Asset button to export all the assets selected in the Export For Screens dialog box.

7   Choose File > Save to save the document and File > Close to close it.

Congratulations! You finished the chapter! Understanding how to create content in Illustrator and how to generate web images from that artwork will serve you well in your design career. Print and web continues to coexist and overlap in many different areas, and having the knowledge to work with both is a huge asset. Keep it up!

CHAPTER OBJECTIVES

Chapter Learning Objectives

- Hone your creativity.
- Prepare your mind for design.
- Apply the design hierarchy.
- Discover the elements of art.
- Understand the element of shape.
- Learn how color works.
- Explore typography.
- Understand the principles of design.

Chapter ACA Objectives

For full descriptions of the objectives, see the table on pages 196–204.

DOMAIN 1.0
WORKING IN THE DESIGN INDUSTRY
1.5, 1.5a, 1.5b, 1.5c

CHAPTER 7

Leveling Up with Design

Now that you have a good grasp of the tools in Adobe Illustrator CC, you'll start learning how best to use them. Much like any other skill, understanding how a tool works and becoming a master craftsperson are two completely different levels of achievement. In many ways, they're distinct ways of thinking about the tools you've learned to use.

★ *ACA Objective 1.5*

As an example, think about carpenters. Their initial level of learning covers tools such as a saw, hammer, and drill. They learn how to use the tools correctly and when to apply specific techniques, including cutting with or against the grain and joining the wood at the joints. Using the right techniques, carpenters can theoretically build anything.

▶ *Video 7.1* *Design School: Introduction*

You're now at the point at which the only way to get better is to practice and learn the thought processes that a master craftsperson goes through to create amazing, creative, and unique work. The beauty of this stage is that it's when you start to become an artist. Being good at using any tool is not just about knowing how it works and what it does. It's knowing *when* to use it and what techniques to apply to create something new.

Creativity Is a Skill

▶ **Video 7.2** *Design School: Creativity Is a Skill*

We discussed creativity in the first chapter of this book, and I'd like to share a little more about it. Let's look back at the highly scientific and statistically accurate diagram that I used before to illustrate the point (**Figure 7.1**).

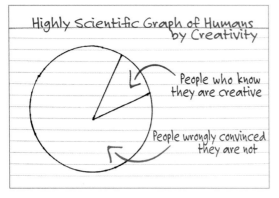

Figure 7.1 Graph of human creativity

Okay, so perhaps the diagram isn't exactly statistically accurate and maybe my methods weren't scientific, but it's still true. Creativity is a skill that you can learn and improve with practice. But there's only one way to guarantee that you'll never be more creative than you are now: giving up.

The biggest creative problem some people have is that they give up. Some give up before even making their first effort. Others give up after their fifth effort or after 15 minutes of not creating a masterpiece. Nobody creates a 15-minute masterpiece. A big difference between a great artist and a terrible one is that a great artist has tried and failed, made some adjustments, and tried again. The next try may also lead to failure, but the artist pushes forward. The artist isn't deterred by bumping into a problem because it's all part of the learning and creative process.

Of course, you can't know how far you can take your creative skills until you start practicing and expanding those skills. But if you never use them, they'll only grow weaker. Remember that every effort, every new attempt, and every goof-up builds strength.

Getting a Creative Workout

This chapter is about developing your creative skills and flexing your creative muscles. It's about turning the craft of being a visual designer into a natural ability. Even if you take the big step of becoming an Adobe Certified Associate, you need to realize that passing the test is just getting through the tryouts. When you get that credential, it's like being picked to be on a professional football team. It's certainly something to be proud of, but the real goal is the Super Bowl! You have a lot more work ahead, but it's fun and rewarding work.

This book introduces you to exercises that help you explore and enhance the skills you already have. Getting beyond the basics of creativity and design is just a matter of applying your existing skills in ways you've never tried. That's all there is to creativity.

Prepping Your Mind

Preparing your mind is the most important part of increasing your creative skills. For most of us, it's also the hardest because today's culture is so focused on instant success and efficiency that people learn to fear the essence of creativity: failure.

Failure—and more specifically, the ability to take failure in stride—is the key ingredient to developing your artistic skillset. This is especially true if you're a beginner and aren't entirely happy with your current abilities. Just face that you're a design baby—and start acting like one!

Yes, I just encouraged you to act like a baby. But I mean an actual infant, not a grown person who is throwing a fit. Babies are fearless and resilient when they fail. They keep trying. They don't give up. Most of the time, they don't even realize that they're failing because they haven't yet learned that concept.

That's what you need to tap into. In art, there are no failures—there are only quitters. Tap into your inner infant! Try and fail, and try and fail, and try and fail. Eventually, you'll take your first step. You may quickly fail again on your second step, but don't give up. Babies don't know that they've failed. They just know that they got *a little bit closer*. They know what every true artist knows and what the rest of us need to remember but have forgotten along the way: *failure is the path*.

The Design Hierarchy

★ *ACA Objective 1.5a*

▶ *Video 7.3 Design School: The Design Hierarchy*

Most of us recognize art when we see it, but nobody can agree on how to create it. In an attempt to provide a framework, artists have developed a list of elements of art, the building blocks of art, and principles of design, the essential rules or assembly instructions of art. Although every artist understands the importance of the elements and principles of art, there is no official list of those elements and principles that all artists agree on. This can be incredibly frustrating. How can you study and learn about something that nobody can fully identify?

Celebrate this fact—the lack of an "official" list means that you can't be wrong. A sculptor and a painter see and approach their art in different ways. A movie producer approaches her art differently than a costume designer approaches his. But all of these artistic people still study and embrace the elements and principles to guide their art.

Applying the Design Hierarchy

★ *ACA Objective 1.5c* The design hierarchy shown in **Figure 7.2** is one way to understand and think about the artistic elements and principles. This isn't the *ultimate* approach to understanding and interacting with the artistic elements and principles. (An "ultimate" approach probably doesn't exist.) It is more of an organized starting place that might help you to focus your design skills.

Figure 7.2 The design hierarchy

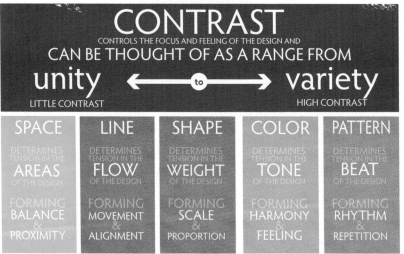

Design, unlike art, generally has a purpose. It's often about creating or accomplishing something specific, rather than simply enjoying or exploring an artistic impulse. A design task might require that you advertise a product, communicate an idea, or promote a cause or specific issue. I find it much easier to think about artistic elements and principles in terms of design, and you can use a design task as a framework on which to "hang" your creative quest when those vague artistic elements and principles seem confusing or muddled.

Thinking through these building blocks can also serve as a great little exercise when you're looking at a piece of work that you're not happy with but can't quite figure out why. Sometimes, just rolling through the following elements and principles in your mind can be an excellent creative checklist.

START WITH A FOCAL POINT

The focal point is what your design is all about. In an advertisement, it's your "call to action" phrase that will motivate the consumer. For a cause, it's the primary message that your cause is trying to get across. In visual design, it could be the navigation elements or the major interactive elements. It's the primary idea that you want people to take with them, like the title of a book or a chapter. It's the "sales pitch" of your design.

The focal point should be the most memorable aspect of the design. In a symmetrical or radial design, centering the focal point will give it the greatest impact. On the other hand, in an asymmetrical design, let it fall on one of the natural focal points, which you'll learn about shortly when you study space.

Critical Question: *Do people know where to look in my design?*

CREATE FOCAL POINTS USING CONTRAST

Contrast creates a focal point by generating "tension" in the image (**Figure 7.3**). Place one red golf ball in a pile of 10,000 white golf balls, and you'll notice it immediately. The most dramatic way to create contrast is to vary the most common characteristic of the elements in the design. If you have a number of multicolored circles that are the same size, then varying the size of one circle, regardless of its color, will create a contrast that draws the eye. Keep the shape the same size, but make it a star instead of a circle to generate the same tension.

Figure 7.3 A focal point is created with contrast: Make one thing different and it stands out.

Establishing unity in a design is essential to allowing you to create tension. Without a degree of unity, you cannot create a focal point and the eye struggles to find something to focus on. Design is about forcing a focal point to be where you want it. When too many different, unrelated elements are present in your design it makes chaos, and the viewer will not know where to look.

Critical Question: Does my design lack sufficient contrast to see the important features clearly?

RANGING FROM UNITY TO VARIETY

Imagine that contrast can be described as the "tension" in the image and that contrast is a range from low contrast, which we call unity, to high contrast, which we call variety. Compositions with very low contrast have very little tension, and these designs are generally perceived as peaceful and calm but can sometimes feel emotionless, cold, and lifeless. Compositions with very high contrast have a lot of tension; they're generally perceived as energetic, lively, active, and hot, but sometimes they feel unpredictable or emotional (**Figure 7.4**).

Figure 7.4 Keep the contrast in your image low toward the unity side unless you're trying to make something stand out.

A Framework for Connecting the Dots

The following framework connects artistic elements and principles to help you at the onset of the creative journey. They're good starting points. Remember that with any design, you're not trying to *define* the artistic elements and principles as much as trying to *embrace* and apply them. As with every study of the artistic elements and principles, you won't arrive at a destination. Rather, you'll embark on a journey. These connections should help you make sense of the elements and principles long enough to find your way to understand and apply them.

CREATE BALANCE AND PROXIMITY BY ARRANGING THE ELEMENTS IN YOUR COMPOSITIONAL SPACE

Tension develops among the various areas of your composition; unify the design with symmetry and equal spacing, or vary it using asymmetry and grouping elements.

Critical Question: Does my design use space to help communicate relationships?

CREATE MOVEMENT AND ALIGNMENT BY ARRANGING YOUR ELEMENTS ALONG LINES

Tension is created with the direction or flow of your composition; unify the design with strict alignment or movement along straight or flowing lines, or vary it with random, chaotic movements away from any single line or flow.

Critical Question: Does my design use lines to communicate order and flow?

CREATE SCALE AND PROPORTION BY CAREFULLY DESIGNING SHAPES IN YOUR COMPOSITION

Tension is created among the sizes of elements in your composition; unify the design with similar or related sizes of elements, or vary it with a mix of unrelated sizes. Keep in mind that a paragraph has a shape, and a group of elements has a shape. Look at areas as well as objects in your design.

Critical Question: Does my design consider the message sent by the size of shapes I create?

CREATE THEMES AND FEELING BY USING TYPOGRAPHY, COLORS, AND VALUES IN YOUR COMPOSITION

Tension is created among elements of different types, values, or colors. Unify the design with related types, colors, and values, or vary it with clashing colors or extreme differences in values or type.

Critical Question: Does my design consider the message sent by the typography, color, and value I used?

USE REPETITION AND RHYTHM TO CREATE PATTERNS AND TEXTURE IN YOUR COMPOSITIONS

Tension is created among elements with different texture or patterns. You can unify design with simple repetition to produce predictable patterns and rhythms, or vary it by using complex, irregular, or chaotic patterns and rhythms.

Critical Question: Does my design consider the message sent by the patterns and textures I designed?

Wrapping Up the Design Hierarchy

If you're familiar with the basic artistic elements and principles, this hierarchy might be a framework you can use. But the goal of art is to continually explore the elements and principles. The next section covers them all, along with some challenges designed to help you dig a little deeper.

The Elements of Art

The **elements of art** (**Figure 7.5**) are the building blocks of creative works. Think of them as the "nouns" of design. The elements are space, line, shape, form, texture, value, color, and type. Many traditional artists leave type off the list, but for graphic designers it is a critical part of how we look at design (and besides that, type is really fun to play with).

Figure 7.5 The elements of art are the building blocks of art and design.

The Element of Space

Space is the first element of art to consider (**Figure 7.6**). It also happens to be one of the most abused, overlooked, neglected, and underrated elements in design. You can look at and consider space in multiple ways.

★ *ACA Objective 1.5c*

▶ **Video 7.5** *Design School: The Element of Space*

Figure 7.6 The element of space

SPACE AS YOUR CANVAS

The most basic way to look at space is as your canvas or working area. In Illustrator, you start a new document and specify its dimensions to create your space. Sometimes the dimensions are specified and provided to you, such as when you're designing for a specific project size or screen resolution. But sometimes you can create a fun way to work by giving yourself an uncommon space to design in.

LEVEL-UP CHALLENGE: A PENNY IN SPACE

Here's a fun challenge:

1 Grab a piece of blank paper, and simply place a coin on it. Don't pick a random place to put it; *design* the spot where it should go.

2 Look at the paper with the coin on it and get a sense for the "feeling" it creates.

3 Fold the paper any way you want, except directly in half, so that you have a differently shaped space, and repeat the process.

Can you see how simply using different sizes and dimensions of space—with the exact same content—can change the way your art "feels"?

And did it enter your mind to fold the paper in a way that wasn't rectangular? Not all spaces have 90-degree corners. Think outside the box…*literally*!

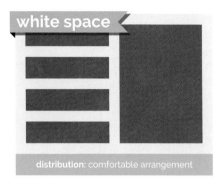

white space

distribution: comfortable arrangement

Figure 7.7 Use space to create comfortable arrangements of elements for your design.

SPACE AS A CREATIVE TOOL

Another important way to look at space is as a design element (**Figure 7.7**). The inability to use space well is an obvious sign of a new designer. A crowded design practically *screams* "newbie"! It takes a while to use space well, and it requires some practice. Start learning to use space as a creative element and you'll see a drastic increase in the artistic feel of your designs.

When used properly, space can provide the following benefits to your designs:

- **Creating emphasis or focus:** When you have space around an object, it tends to give it emphasis. Crowding things makes them seem less important.

- **Creating feeling:** Space can be used to create a feeling of loneliness, isolation, or exclusivity. It can also be used to create a feeling of seriousness or gravitas.

- **Creating visual rest:** Sometimes space is needed to simply create some visual "breathing room" so that the other elements in your design can speak as intended.

THE RULE OF THIRDS

The **rule of thirds** (**Figure 7.8**) is critical in photography and video, and it also applies to all visual arts. To visualize it, think of the rule of thirds like a tic-tac-toe board overlaid onto your design. Two horizontal and two vertical divisions create nine equal boxes on your design. The basic rule is that major elements of your design should fall on the dividing lines, and the areas of emphasis for the design should fall on the intersections. Using this rule in your designs creates compositions that have much more interest, tension, and visual strength.

Figure 7.8 Use the rule of thirds to determine where major elements should fall to create a visually appealing layout.

NEGATIVE SPACE

In the design industry, people use the term negative space, or "white space," to refer to blank areas in the design, even if you're working on a colored background. Negative space (**Figure 7.9**) is one of my favorite creative uses of the element of space. It can be fun to explore using negative space to create clever logos or designs.

Figure 7.9 Negative space isn't wasted; it's *used*.

TIP

You can see an awesome collection of updated examples of negative space online at www.brainbuffet.com/design/negative-space.

Sometimes you can place a boring idea in negative space to get moving in a new, creative direction. It can be tough for beginners to even "see" negative space, but once you look for it, you'll start to see creative uses of it everywhere. Begin to use it, and your design skills will jump up a level.

From here on out, the elements get much easier to understand because we can think of them as things (whereas we tend to think of space as the absence of things, or "nothing"). Learn to use space well. The ability to do so is the mark of an experienced and talented artist.

NOTE

For many people, the terms negative space and white space are interchangeable. If you're unclear about what someone is asking for, seek clarification. Art and design are not entirely technical, accurate, and organized processes, so you'll need to get used to lots of "mushy" terms that are used in multiple ways.

LEVEL-UP CHALLENGE: SKETCHING NOTHING

This simple exercise will help you start to see negative space and learn how to create it.

Place a chair on a table, and then sketch everything you see except the chair. Don't worry if your sketch is messy—this is not about your artistic skill; it's about learning to see. Just focus on learning to see the space around things rather than the things themselves. When you're done, you'll have a chair-shaped hole in your drawing. Notice that the space where you drew nothing has the most visual impact. Space is powerful!

The Element of Line

▶ **Video 7.6** *Design School: The Element of Line*

The meaning of **line** is pretty obvious. Although technical definitions such as "a point moving through a space" exist, we are all aware of what a line is. A line is exactly what you think it is: a mark with a beginning and an end (**Figure 7.10**). Don't overthink the basics. We're going to dig deeper than that, but let's start with the basic idea and then build the new understanding on it.

The line in **Figure 7.10** could easily be created in Illustrator by drawing a path using the Pen or Pencil tool and then varying the width of that path using the Width tool.

Figure 7.10 The element of line

LEVEL-UP CHALLENGE: LINE 'EM UP!

See how many ways you can think about the concept of a line. You'll explore more of these ideas later in this chapter, but first let's see how many different kinds of lines you can draw.

Here are some quick ideas to get you started:

- **Level I:** Short, long, straight, wavy, zigzag, geometric, organic
- **Level II:** Angry, lonely, worried, excited, overjoyed
- **Level III:** Opposition, contrast, politics, infinity

Try to create as many different kinds of lines as you can and find a word to describe each one. There are no wrong answers here; this is art.

Remember, you're just drawing lines, not *pictures*. So to indicate sadness, don't draw an upside down "u." The goal is to draw a line that, in itself, represents sadness. It's a little challenging as you move away from descriptions and closer to abstract ideas, but that's the point. The best artists learn to "hint" at feelings and concepts in their art. Explore!

COMMON LINE DESCRIPTORS

The following qualities are often associated with lines, and thinking about the ways lines are used or drawn can help you determine the meaning that your lines are giving to your design.

- **Direction** (**Figure 7.11**): The direction of the lines in your art implies certain feelings or subconscious messages. **Vertical** lines tend to express power and elevation, whereas **horizontal** lines tend to express calm and balance. **Diagonal** lines often express growth or decline, and they imply movement or change.

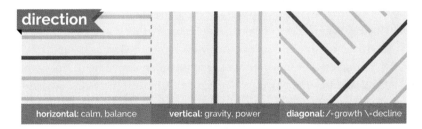

Figure 7.11 Line direction can communicate feeling in your designs.

- **Weight** (**Figure 7.12**): The weight of a line describes its thickness. Heavy or thick lines generally represent importance and strength, and they tend to feel more masculine. Light or thin lines generally communicate delicacy and elegance, and they tend to represent femininity.

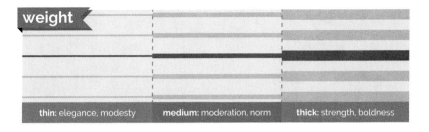

Figure 7.12 The weight of your lines communicates different feelings or concepts as well.

- **Style** (**Figure 7.13**): A line style is an effect, such as a double line or dotted line. Varying-width lines are useful for expressing flow and grace. Hand-drawn lines look as if they were created with traditional media such as paints, charcoal, or chalk. Implied lines are lines that don't really exist—like dotted or dashed lines, or the lines we create when we line up at the grocery checkout. These implied lines are powerful tools for designers; individual things can feel unified or grouped together when they are aligned (you'll find out more about implied lines in a moment).

Figure 7.13 Line styles are the most popular way to communicate feeling.

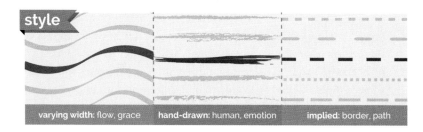

- **Flow:** We've created this word for the category that is related to the energy conveyed by lines and shapes. Geometric lines tend to be straight and have sharp angles; they look manmade and intentional. Geometric lines communicate strength, power, and precision when used in design. Curved lines express fluidity, beauty, and grace. Organic lines are usually irregular and imperfect—the kind of lines you find in nature or as the result of random processes. Organic lines represent nature, movement, and elegance. Chaotic lines look like scribble and feel unpredictable and frantic. They convey a sense of urgency, fear, or explosive energy (**Figure 7.14**).

Figure 7.14 Line flow can communicate energy.

- **Implied lines:** If you look at the leftmost line of these paragraphs, you can see a "line" formed by the beginning of each line of type. Pay attention to the implied lines you create using the design elements in your artwork. Think of creative ways to use and suggest lines, and pay attention to what you might be saying with them. Make sure that the message all your lines send matches the intent of your work. Implied lines are similar to negative space; learning to work with them can boost your design skills exponentially (**Figure 7.15**).

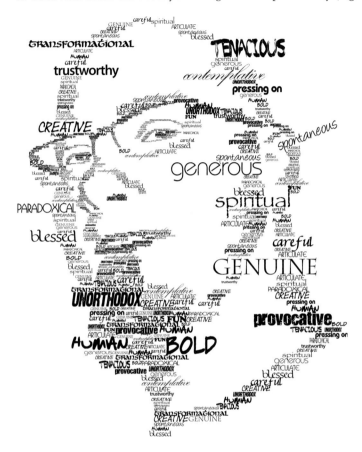

Figure 7.15 Typographic portraits are excellent examples of the use of implied lines. Note how you can "see" the image of a face, even though there is nothing but carefully arranged text.

The Element of Shape

The next element needs little introduction: shape (**Figure 7.16**) can be defined as an area enclosed or defined by an outline.

▶ *Video 7.7 Design School: The Element of Shape*

Figure 7.16 The element of shape

We're familiar with shapes such as circles, squares, and triangles, but there are many more shapes than that. Those specific shapes are created in geometry, but what about the shape of a hand or cloud (**Figure 7.17**)? These are shapes too, and we often use the same descriptors for shapes as we do lines.

Figure 7.17 Be aware of the feelings conveyed by the shapes you use.

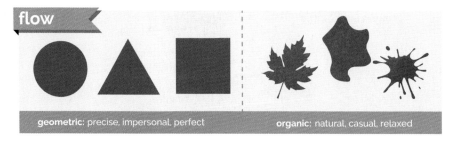

REPRESENTATIVE SHAPES

A **pictograph** (or **pictogram**) is a graphic symbol that represents something in the real world (**Figure 7.18**). Computer icons are pictographs that often suggest the function they represent (like a trash can icon to delete a file). Other examples of pictographs are the human silhouettes often used to indicate men's and women's restrooms. They're not *accurate* representations of the real objects, but they are *clear* representations of them. **Ideographs** (or **ideograms**) are images that represent an idea. A heart shape represents love, a lightning bolt represents electricity, or a question mark represents being puzzled. **Representative shapes** are helpful in communicating across language barriers and can be valuable when you are designing for multicultural and multilingual audiences.

Figure 7.18
Representative shapes

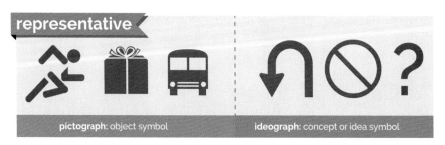

The Element of Form

Form (**Figure 7.19**) describes three-dimensional objects or, at least, objects that look 3D. The best way to visualize form clearly is to consider that circles, squares, and triangles are shapes, whereas spheres, cubes, and pyramids are forms. Like shapes, forms are basically divided into geometric and organic types. Geometric forms, such as a cube, are common to us. We are also familiar with organic forms such as the human form or the form of a peanut. When you work with 3D in applications, these forms are often referred to as "solids."

▶ *Video 7.8* *Design School: The Element of Form*

Figure 7.19 The element of form

3D LIGHTING

In art and design, we place a special focus on the techniques that make images appear 3D in a 2D work of art. Although not covered in this book, you should know that Adobe Illustrator contains tools that allow you to create 3D shapes from 2D objects that you draw. You have some standard elements to consider when you want to create a feeling of depth and form. **Figure 7.20** explains the standard elements of a 3D drawing.

- **Highlight**: The area of a form directly facing the light; appears lightest.
- **Object shadow**: The area of the form that is facing away from the light source; appears darkest.
- **Cast shadow**: The shadow cast on the ground and on any objects that are in the shadow of the form. One thing to remember is that shadows fade as they get farther from the form casting the shadow. Be sure to take this into account as you're creating shadow effects in your art.
- **Light source**: The perceived location of the lighting in relation to the form.
- **Reflected highlight**: The area of the form that is lit by reflections from the ground or other objects in the scene. This particular element of drawing a 3D object is most often ignored but provides believable lighting on the object.

Figure 7.20 Elements of 3D design

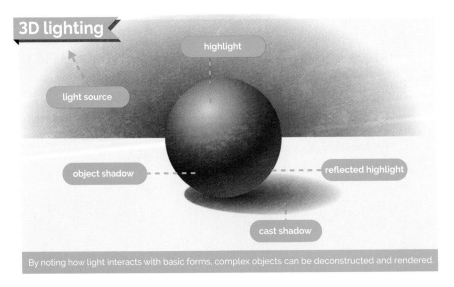

This is a standard art exercise. You might ask a friend in an art class or an art teacher to help with this one, or find a tutorial online. You'll draw a sphere with lighting and shadow on a flat plane. Imagine a cue ball on a white table. Be sure to include the elements mentioned in this section and shown in the example of 3D lighting.

Your sketch might not be great. In fact, it may be horrible. If it's your first time and it looks better than you could do in kindergarten, you're doing well. Although you've got digital tools to help with this stuff, learning to draw and doodle activates a different part of your brain, and you want to wake up that part. I'm more concerned with you learning the ideas than mastering 3D drawing on paper.

Focus on learning how things look and how to represent them in art and design. And look at some real 3D objects in the light. Put a tennis ball on the sidewalk and just stare at it. It's amazing how much of the real world you never pay attention to! Art is more about learning to see than learning to draw or create.

The Elements of Pattern and Texture

Pattern (**Figure 7.21**) can be defined as a repetitive sequence of colors, shapes, or values. Pattern is technically a different concept from texture, but in graphic design it's often regarded as the same thing. Let's face it: all of our "textures" are just ink on paper or pixels. Any repetitive texture might also be considered a pattern. (Think of "diamond plate" or "tile" textures. They're just a pattern of Xs or squares.) In Chapter 4, for example, you created a pattern and applied it to a shape as part of the business card project.

▶ *Video 7.9*
Design School: The Elements of Pattern and Texture

Figure 7.21 The elements of pattern and texture

Texture (**Figure 7.22**) can describe an actual, tactile texture in real objects or the appearance of texture in a 2D image. It's important to use texture to communicate feeling and authenticity in your art or designs. If you want to depict something elegant, soft, or comfortable, you could use a texture that resembles fabric or clouds. To represent strength or power, you might choose textures that represent stone or metal. And you could represent casual, informal, or nostalgic feelings using a texture that represents weathered wood or worn paint. To that end, in Chapter 5 you used a woodgrain image to add texture to text on the music poster.

Figure 7.22 Texture and feeling

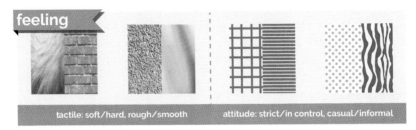

As you work more as a designer, you'll start to notice the nuances and subtle differences between textures and patterns. For now, just think of them as the visual qualities of your shapes and forms that can't be described by color and/or value alone.

LEVEL-UP CHALLENGE: TEXTURE TANGLE

Texture is a valuable design tool. The goal of this exercise is to experiment with texture and patterns. Remember that it takes practice to create things on paper the way you visualize them in your head, but that's the life of an artist. It's never perfect; it's just art.

1 Grab a sheet of paper and a fine-point pen.
2 Draw a line that crosses over itself at least once, forming a loop that goes from one edge of the paper to another. That loop is your first "texture pit."
3 In that loop, create a texture by just repeating a pattern.
4 Create another area and fill it with a different pattern or texture.

That's it! When your paper is full, you have leveled up.

- **Level I:** Use only geometric textures and patterns.
- **Level II:** Attempt to create areas that look like textures of materials, plants, or animals. You might need to switch to pencil to be able to shade the areas well.
- **Level III:** Introduce color. Try adding color to your designs and see how that works.

The Element of Value

Value (**Figure 7.23**) describes the lightness or darkness of an object. Together with color, value represents the entire visible spectrum. You can think of value as a gradient that goes from black to white. But remember that value applies to color as well, and you can have a spectrum that fades from black, through a color, and then to white. From this comes the idea of a "red black" or a "blue black" introducing a hint of color to your blacks (**Figure 7.24**). You'll explore that concept later in this chapter.

▶ *Video 7.10* *Design School: The Element of Value*

Figure 7.23 The element of value

Figure 7.24 Ranges of value in several colors

Professionals in the art and design industry sometimes use the term *value*, but clients rarely use it. Clients will just ask you to lighten or darken a graphic or text, or sometimes use tint, shade, or tone in place of value. Technically, these terms are different, but many people use tone, shade, tint, and value interchangeably. As always, when clients use a term and you're not exactly sure what they mean, ask for clarification. Sometimes clients don't know exactly what they mean, so asking ensures that everyone is on the same page.

The Element of Color

▶ *Video 7.11*
Design School:
The Element of
Color

When you think about it, **color** is hard to define. How would you define color without using examples of colors? Check out its definition in a dictionary and you'll find that defining color doesn't help you understand it. Color is best *experienced* and *explored* (**Figure 7.25**).

Figure 7.25 The element of color

We have so many ways to think about color and so many concepts to dig into that exploring color is a lifelong pursuit for most artists and designers. Color theory is a deep and complex study. You'll explore the basics here, but remember that this is just the on-ramp to understanding color. Grasp these concepts and you'll still have a lot more to learn.

Color psychology is a relatively new discipline and an interesting study that focuses on the emotional and behavioral effects that colors have on people. The colors you choose really do matter. For our purposes, we'll define color as the perceived hue, lightness, and saturation of an object or light.

HOW COLOR WORKS

Color is created in two ways: combining light to create additive color and subtracting light to create subtractive color (**Figure 7.26**). In Illustrator, the color mode you select will define how the color is created.

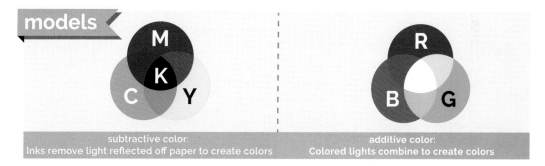

Figure 7.26 Subtractive and additive color

Additive color is created by combining light. This is how your monitor, digital camera, and mobile phone work. The most common color mode for additive color is RGB. The letters RGB stand for red, green, and blue, which are the three colors used to create digital images. Monitors and electronic devices are dark when turned off, and you create colors by adding light to the screen.

Subtractive color is created by subtracting light. This is the color system you learned in early art classes in which red, blue, and yellow were the primary colors. For print, we use CMYK, which refers to the colors of ink used in standard color printing: cyan, magenta, yellow, and black. We start with a white surface (the paper) that reflects all the light back to us. Then we subtract color by using paints or inks that limit the light that is reflected back to the viewer. Colors created this way are called process colors.

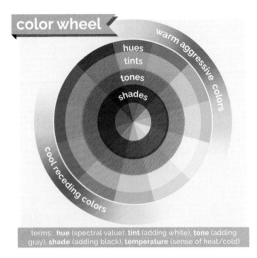

terms: **hue** (spectral value), **tint** (adding white), **tone** (adding gray), **shade** (adding black), **temperature** (sense of heat/cold)

Figure 7.27 The color wheel

primary colors—cannot be created by mixing
secondary—mix 2 primary colors
tertiary—mix primary and secondary colors

Figure 7.28 How secondary and tertiary colors are built

THE COLOR WHEEL

Sir Isaac Newton invented the color wheel (**Figure 7.27**) in the mid-17th century. The color wheel offers a way to display and build all the colors possible using paint. It's a common exercise in beginning art classes to create a color wheel when learning to mix and experiment with colors. In digital imaging, it's not as important to go through this exercise, but if you have a chance, give it a try. It's interesting to see how all of the colors can mix to obtain the infinite colors and shades the human eye can perceive.

The color wheel is important because many color theories we use are named after their relative positions on the color wheel. They're a lot easier to remember if we use the color wheel to illustrate.

The first thing to realize is that some colors are classified as primary colors. These colors can be combined to create every other color in the visible spectrum. For subtractive color used in traditional art, the primary colors are red, blue, and yellow. For additive colors, the primary colors are red, blue, and green.

The colors that are created when you combine primary colors are called secondary colors because you can create them only by applying a second step of mixing the colors. When we mix secondary and primary colors, we get another set of colors known as tertiary colors. **Figure 7.28** illustrates how these colors are built.

LEVEL-UP CHALLENGE: GET ROLLING WITH COLOR

Creating a color wheel is a staple project in art classes. Any experienced traditional artist or art teacher can help you with this task. You can find a ton of information about this online, but this is a valuable project to help you get in touch with color and understand how colors are related.

- **Level I:** Create a traditional color wheel using paint on paper.
- **Level II:** Create a CMYK color wheel in Illustrator.

BASIC COLOR RULES

Color rules (also called color harmonies) are a great way to start picking colors for your design projects. The color rules (**Figure 7.29**) are all named for their relative locations on the color wheel. We're going to cover some of the basic color rules and the impressions they tend to communicate.

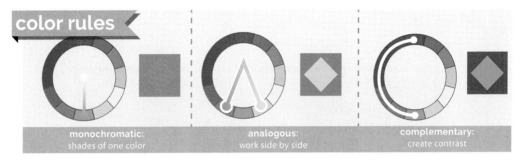

Figure 7.29 Color rules

The three most common ways of thinking about colors (and, really, the basis of all color rules) are monochromatic, analogous, and complementary color schemes.

- **Monochromatic**: Monochromatic colors, as you've probably guessed, are based only on different shades and tints of the same color. They tend to communicate a relaxed and peaceful feeling, and you'll create little contrast or energy in art using these colors.

- **Analogous**: If you want to add a little more variation while maintaining a calm feeling, consider analogous colors. Analogous colors sit side by side on the color wheel, and they tend to create gentle and relaxing color schemes. Analogous colors don't usually stand out from each other; they seem to work together and can almost disappear together when overlaid.

- **Complementary**: Complementary colors are opposite each other on the color wheel. Complementary color combinations are high in contrast and normally very vibrant, so use with caution. When overused, complementary color can be very "loud" and can easily cross over into visually obnoxious if you're not careful. You can remember this rule with the alliterative phrase "Complementary colors create contrast."

If you want to explore color combinations, visit *color.adobe.com* and explore the Adobe Color CC website (**Figure 7.30**). It's an amazing way to browse other people's color collections or grab colors from an image you like and create a color set to use for your projects. When you register with your free Adobe ID, you can save the color themes you find or create and bring them into your Adobe apps to use and share with others.

Adobe Color is also part of a free app for iOS and Android. Open the Adobe Capture CC app (**Figure 7.31**) and select Colors, open an image or point your phone camera at something, and create a color theme. Experiment with creating custom themes from your favorite blanket, a sunset, your goldfish, or your crazy uncle's tie-dyed concert shirt from Woodstock.

Figure 7.30 Use the Adobe Color CC website to explore color harmonies and save combinations to your Creative Cloud account.

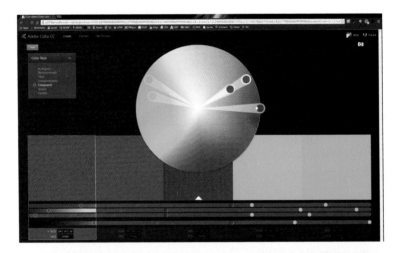

Figure 7.31 The Adobe Capture CC app lets you capture colors from photos you've taken or grab them live using the camera.

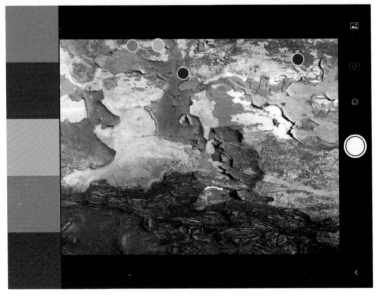

COLOR ASSOCIATIONS

We tend to associate different things with different colors. As a designer you must learn to recognize and properly use the right color for the message you want to convey. Again, this isn't a science, and you'll need to consider more than this chart when developing your color-picking strategies. But understanding colors and their associations (**Figure 7.32**) can be useful to produce the right "feel" in your images. You can evoke interesting feelings and contrasts by capitalizing on these associations in your interactive design work.

associations

sky, water, peace, cold

nature, growth, money

sunlight, joy, energy

fire, warmth, attention

blood, passion, danger

flowers, creativity

Color associations can depend on culture, profession, or experience.

Figure 7.32 Common color associations

The Element of Type

Type (**Figure 7.33**) is generally not considered a traditional element of art, but it can be a critical part of your work as a designer. Typefaces carry a lot of emotional meaning, and choosing the proper typefaces for a job is a skill that every designer needs (yet many don't have). Like color, this area of design is so deep and has so many aspects that entire books and college courses are focused only on typography. We can't reduce it to simple rules such as "Use three typefaces, maximum. When in doubt use Helvetica. And never use Chiller." (Even though that's not a bad starting point!)

Figure 7.33 The element of type

Working with type is often like being a marriage counselor or matchmaker. Every typeface has a personality, and you need to carefully match the type in your design work so it has a compatible relationship with the overall feeling of the piece. The typefaces you use also need to work together. It takes time and experience to master this balance, but over time you can become a skillful typeface matchmaker. Most artists have a few fonts they tend to lean on heavily, and that's okay—especially at the beginning.

★ *ACA Objective 1.5b*

▶ *Video 7.12 Design School: The Element of Type*

 TIP

Check online at www.brainbuffet.com/design/typography for a list of fonts and typography-based resources to help you dig a little deeper with this concept.

TYPOGRAPHY

Typography is the art of using letterforms and type arrangement to help the language communicate a message. As mentioned earlier, type can be its own topic of study and can easily get overwhelming. We'll skim the surface here but hope that as you move forward in your design, you'll dig a little deeper. Let's get some vocabulary out of the way first.

Technically, a typeface (**Figure 7.34**) is the letterform set that makes up the type. Helvetica, Arial, Garamond, and Chiller are examples of typefaces. In brief, it's the "look" of the letters. A font is a specific collection of characters from the typeface in each of its sizes and styles. So 12 pt. Arial Narrow and 12 pt. Arial Bold are different *fonts* of the same *typeface*. The same is true for two different sizes of the same typeface.

Figure 7.34 Many of today's typography terms were created in the days of movable type and have changed as publishing technology has evolved.

Font files for your computer generally contain all sizes of a particular typeface in a single style, like bold, italic, or condensed. Having a set of font files that have multiple styles is often called having a "font family" for that particular typeface.

From now on, let's use the term *font*, because that's also the name of the file you'll install when you add typefaces to your computer, and it's the most common term. Few people will bother splitting hairs in these differences that really don't exist anymore for computer-generated type.

TYPE CLASSIFICATIONS

There are many different ways to classify typefaces, but we'll rely on the Adobe Typekit classifications for the purpose of this chapter (you worked with Typekit fonts in Chapter 2). Generally, people divide fonts into two main categories of type that should be used for large areas of type: serif and sans-serif (**Figure 7.35**).

- **Serif fonts** are often associated with typewritten documents and most printed books. Generally, serif fonts are considered to be easier to read in larger paragraphs of text. Because so many books use serif fonts and early typewriters produced them, serif text often feels a bit more traditional, intelligent, and classy.

- **Sans serif fonts** do not include serifs. "Sans" is a French word that migrated to English and simply means "without." Sans serif fonts are often used for headlines and titles for their strong, stable, modern feel. Sans serif fonts are also preferred for large areas of text for reading on websites and screen reading.

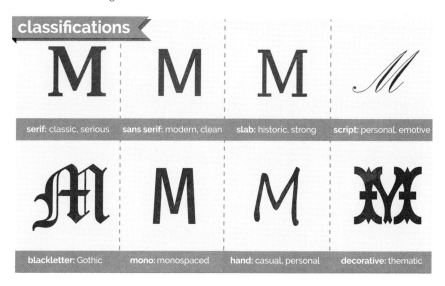

Figure 7.35 Typeface classifications used by Adobe

Beyond these basic types of text we use in our documents, designers use other type-faces that are not appropriate for large areas of type because they're not easy to read in a long paragraph. Most designers consider the following fonts to be "decorative" for that reason.

- **Slab serif fonts** (also called Egyptian, block serif, or square serif) are a more squared-off version of a typical serif font. These fonts bridge the gap between serif and sans serif fonts and generally feel a bit more machine-built. The simple design tends to make them feel a bit rougher than their serif counterparts.

- **Script fonts** (also called formal or calligraphical) have an elegant feeling. These fonts are great to use for invitations to formal events, such as weddings, and in designs where you want to convey a feeling of beauty, grace, and/or feminine dignity. If you are designing for a spa, for a beauty shop, or for products or services, script fonts will carry a feeling of relaxed and elegant beauty.

- **Blackletter fonts** (also called old English, Gothic, or textura) feature an overly ornate style and are often used to title formal documents such as certificates, diplomas, or degrees, as well as old German Bibles and heavy metal bands. It conveys a feeling of rich and sophisticated gravitas, often hinting at a long history of tradition and reliability.

- **Monospaced fonts** (also called fixed-width or nonproportional) use the same amount of horizontal space for each letter. Typically, fonts use a variable spacing technique called kerning. (You'll learn more about kerning later in this chapter.) Monospaced fonts, in contrast, use the same width for every character. Monospaced fonts are good to use when you're trying to make something look impersonal, machine-generated, or retro-geeky because typewriters and early computers used monospaced fonts.

- **Handwritten fonts** (also called hand fonts) simulate handwriting. They are popular for adding a personalized, casual, or human touch to your designs and are often used on junk mail to try to trick you into opening that "Special limited time offer just for you!" (don't fall for it). Handwritten fonts are prefect for communicating casual and friendly feelings, but they can be tough to read in a larger block of text.

- **Decorative fonts** (also called ornamental, novelty, or display) don't fall into any of the other categories. They also tend to convey specific feelings. Decorative fonts should be used sparingly and intentionally. Never use a novelty font just because you think it looks cool; that's a typical newbie move. Make sure you are striving to convey something specific when using decorative fonts.

TIP

Want to create a font based on your own handwriting? Go to www.calligraphr.com to create a font from your handwriting for free.

NOTE

Each character of a font, whether it's a letter, number, symbol, or swash, is called a glyph.

- **Dingbat fonts** (also called wingdings) are a special type of font that doesn't have an alphabet but instead consists of a collection of shapes or objects.

TYPE TALK

You'll need to learn a lot of jargon concerning type when working in the design industry. Some of it is commonly used in discussion about design, and some of it will help you discuss fonts when you're trying to find the perfect typeface for your design.

TYPOGRAPHIC ANATOMY

Figure 7.36 illustrates many of the anatomical terms used when discussing typography. Software has no settings for these options, so we won't go into detail about them. When you start to study typography and learn these terms, you will more easily discern the differences between typefaces. It's easiest to understand these terms by simply looking at the illustration. You will hear these terms in the industry, and when you're looking for a specific font, knowing these terms will allow you to more easily describe what you're looking for. Let's face it: you can't get too far professionally if you're always using words like "doohickey" and "little hangy-downy thingy." These terms are descriptive, like ascenders and descenders; anthropomorphic, like arms, shoulders, and tails; or architectural, like counters and finials.

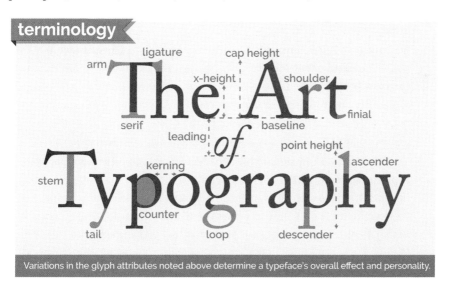

Figure 7.36 Many key typographical terms are illustrated in this image.

THE HOLY TRINITY OF TYPOGRAPHY

Three main concepts of typography exist: kerning, leading, and tracking, known as "The Trinity of Typography" (**Figure 7.37**). As a designer, you need to master these concepts. The terms defined here affect the ways that the letters are spaced from each other vertically or horizontally.

Figure 7.37 Kerning, tracking, and leading—the Trinity of Typography

- **Kerning** is the space between specific letter pairs. For example, the first two letters in the word "Too" are closer than the first two letters in the word "The" because the letter "o" can tuck under the crossbar of the "T." A high-quality font file will have a good set of kerning pairs for specific letter combinations, but for some professional work (and with poorly designed fonts) you might need to get in there and tweak the kerning. Adjusting the kerning between specific letters can help you perfect your type presentation in logos and headlines.

- **Tracking** is the overall space between all the letters in a block of text. It allows you to compress or expand the space between the letters as a whole, rather than just between specific pairs as you do with kerning. Adjusting tracking can greatly affect the feeling that text conveys. Experiment with tracking to help create various feelings in headlines and titles.

- **Leading** is the amount of space between the baselines of two lines of text. The **baseline** is the imaginary line that text sits on. Whereas word processing applications tend to limit you to single and double-line spacing, professional design software lets you manipulate the leading to set a specific distance between multiple lines of text. Doing so can create great-looking space in a design or even overlap with your paragraph text. Experiment with this option in your work. You can change the mood of text by adjusting only the leading of a paragraph.

SIZE, SCALE, AND SMALL CAPS

The terms that appear in **Figure 7.38** are available in the Character panel of the interface for most Adobe design applications.

- Type size is traditionally the height from the highest ascender to the lowest descender in a font, expressed in points (1/72 of an inch). Today, it's more of a guideline than a firm definition, so most designers set the appropriate type size by eye. Different fonts of the same point size can appear to be much different in physical size if the ascenders and descenders are different from each other.

- Vertical and horizontal scale are terms that describe the function of stretching letters and distorting the typeface geometry. Because they distort the typeface, use them with caution. They should be used only when you are trying to express a specific feeling and should not be used in blocks of type because readability can suffer with either of these adjustments.

- All caps and small caps are similar in that they both use only the uppercase letterforms for each letter, but ALL CAPS makes all the letters the same size, whereas small caps sets the letters that would normally be capitalized at a larger size. Small caps tend to increase readability compared to all caps, but both cap formats should be avoided in large blocks of text because they are more difficult to read than standard text.

- Ligatures and swashes are special alternative settings offered with some fonts to combine letters or add stylized touches to certain letter combinations or letters. For example, when the "Th" combination touches in a headline, you can replace it with a single ligature that looks much better. Swashes add flowing and elegant endings to letters with ascenders and descenders. Both of these are normally reserved for type that is expressing an especially elegant or artistic feel.

> **TIP**
>
> *Higher-end typefaces may provide a small caps face that is much nicer than using the setting in software. If this is critical for your design, look for a font that supports this feature.*

> **NOTE**
>
> *The settings for ligatures and swashes are available in the Open-Type panel of most Adobe design apps but not in the Character panel. These rarely used features can lend creative expression to fonts that support it.*

Figure 7.38 Size and special characters

PARAGRAPH SETTINGS

Paragraph settings affect an entire paragraph, rather than selected words (**Figure 7.39**). These options adjust the alignment of the paragraph: left, centered, or right. Justified text aligns a straight edge on both edges of the paragraph with the ability to dictate how the last line is aligned. Indent settings let you choose how far the entire paragraph is indented on each side or in just its first line. Paragraph spacing settings are similar to leading but apply to paragraphs—instead of lines of type within them—and you also can set the space above or below paragraphs. Hyphenation allows you to determine if and when words should be split with hyphenation.

Figure 7.39 The icons for the paragraph settings are quite helpful in illustrating the function of each setting.

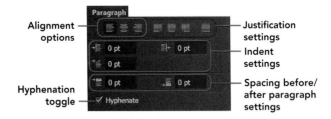

Wrapping Up the Elements

As you've seen in this chapter, the elements are the building blocks or the raw materials of design. But what turns these elements into art is applying the principles of design to the way you arrange these elements in your project. In the next section, you'll explore these principles, which are a framework that help you arrange your work in an artistic way.

The Principles of Design

Much like the elements of design, different artists and schools of thought will generate different ideas about what makes up the principles of design (**Figure 7.40**). For a young artist, this can be frustrating. Sometimes you just want someone to tell you the answer.

★ *ACA Objective 1.5a*

▶ **Video 7.13** *Design School: The Principles of Design*

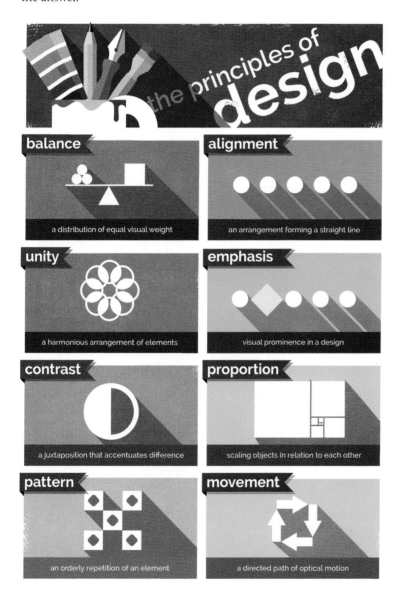

Figure 7.40 Principles of design

But after you understand the principles, you'll appreciate that no one can point to a universal list of artistic principles. If there's no correct answer, there's also no *wrong* answer either. Creatively, you always have another way to approach your art, and becoming an artist doesn't mean that you learn to see any one approach. Becoming an artist means that you learn to *see*.

Until you explore design principles, you will not be ready to understand them. Therefore, definitions are not as helpful as hands-on work. But truly grasping the principles and experiencing them is the only way to grow as an artist. This is the beginning of a lifelong exploration of beauty and creativity.

The bottom line is this: don't get hung up on names or descriptions. Try to engage with each idea as a loosely formed concept that remains fluid and flexible rather than defining boundaries. By studying principles, you're trying to do just the opposite—moving in directions that have no boundaries. The goal of all good art and design is to explore new ways to use the elements and principles, and not to repeat what's been done in the past. You'll examine these principles to start your understanding of something, not to limit it.

The Principles of Emphasis or Focal Point

▶ *Video 7.14*
Design School:
The Principle of
Emphasis

Emphasis (**Figure 7.41**) describes the focal point to which the eye is naturally and initially drawn in a design. Some art has a focus that's obvious. Most marketing and advertising is that way. Other art invites you to step in and explore. It might encourage an exploration of color or texture, but it has no specific point other than the color or texture.

Figure 7.41 Emphasis creates the focal point—a place where the eye is naturally drawn when encountering the image. Use this to your advantage when designing.

Think of emphasis as the main point or primary idea in a piece of art. You can move the viewer's eye to a specific point in the design by making something *different*. You can easily find examples right on the pages of this book. Chapter headings are larger than the rest of the type. Glossary terms are a different color. Even the simple process of *italicizing* words or putting them in **boldface** makes text stand out. The human eye is naturally drawn to unique things. If you want to make something stand out, make it different.

Careful use of contrast is critical to master because a typical design newbie tries to make everything special and unique. As a result, nothing stands out. The design looks *random*, not cool. Give a piece some unity, and it will feel right. You can then emphasize what's truly important.

The Principle of Contrast

Contrast generally creates visual interest and a focal point in a composition. If you think about it, a blank canvas is a canvas with no contrast. As soon as you begin to alter the surface and create contrast, you also start to create a focus. The principle of contrast can be defined as a difference in the qualities of the elements in an image. To use contrast is to create something different from the surrounding pieces of the composition.

▶ *Video 7.15*
Design School: The Principle of Contrast

Many artists limit their understanding of contrast by confining it to color or value. But contrast is much more than that. Any difference between one thing and another creates contrast. You can have contrast in size, texture, value, color, or any of the defining characteristics you learned about in exploring the elements.

The most important thing to remember about contrast is that all contrast creates some emphasis, and if you have too much emphasis, you will have no focal point.

The Principle of Unity

Unity generally communicates calm, peaceful, or cool feelings in your art. The principle of unity (also called harmony) requires that the things that go together ought to *look* like they belong together (**Figure 7.42**). The elements in your design should feel like a family. This doesn't necessarily mean that everything needs to be the same—just that they should share some similar traits. When you have no unity, you can have no focal point and, therefore, no emphasis.

▶ *Video 7.16*
Design School: The Principle of Unity

Figure 7.42 The similar lines, colors, and even values of this image give it a unified feeling.

Note the headings of the different sections in this chapter. They make it easy to find the content you are looking for when skimming the book. Even the breaks between paragraphs help distinguish one concept from another. But all of the words in this paragraph belong together because they share a unity of typeface, spacing, color, and so on.

Unity is important in your compositions so that when you create contrast it draws the viewer's eye where you want it to go. In design, more than in art, we are interested in guiding a viewer's perceptions. Design generally tends to be much more intentional than art. Both are important, however, and beginning with design can make your experimentation with artistic elements and principles much more effective and productive.

The Principle of Variety

▶ *Video 7.17*
Design School:
The Principle of
Variety

Variety tends to communicate energy, heat, and high emotion in a design. When applying the principle of variety, you use different elements in an image to create visual interest. In many ways, it is the exact opposite of unity. You can think of unity and variety as being at the opposite ends of contrast. Unity is establishing a low degree of contrast in a composition. Variety does the opposite and brings a higher amount of contrast to the composition.

Variety is a principle that normally needs to be used sparingly. Too much variety quickly moves your art from interesting to chaotic and disorganized (**Figure 7.43**). Beginning artists and designers sometimes have a hard time properly using variety. They get a bit carried away and lose all sense of focus or unity. Beware of that tendency!

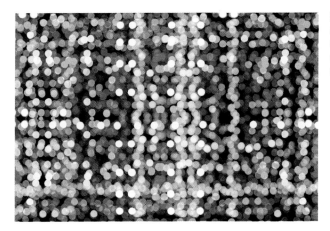

Figure 7.43 When everything is different in an image like these colored lights are, nothing stands out.

The Principle of Balance

Balance suggests the arrangement of things in an image should not be evenly distributed. This is not to say that everything should be centered and that placing something in the top right means you should mirror it with something similar in the top left. That's how a nondesigner lays out a composition. Experienced artists learn to properly balance all of the elements—including space—in their compositions.

Balance comes in many forms: symmetrical, asymmetrical, or radial.

- **Symmetrical:** Symmetrical balance is what most students latch on to at first. It occurs when you can divide an image along its middle and the left side of the image is a mirror image of its right (or the top reflects the bottom). Using a seesaw analogy, a symmetrical balance would have two equally sized people equally distant from the fulcrum. This is the easiest balance to execute, but it conveys a very intentional, formal, and mechanical feeling.

- **Asymmetrical:** Asymmetrical balance (**Figure 7.44**) achieves balance with different elements on each side (or the top and bottom) of an image. Imagine an adult on a seesaw with a child. They can balance, but only if the adult is closer to the fulcrum and the child is farther away. To achieve asymmetrical balance, you need to use space to counterbalance the different weights on each side.

▶ *Video 7.18*
Design School: The Principle of Balance

TIP

Many artists and designers characterize pieces that are out of balance as "leaning to the left," "leaning to the right," or "top-heavy." Over time, you'll develop these feelings too and be able to spot when art seems like it might physically tip over.

Figure 7.44 This image, though asymmetrical, is well balanced. The bright sun is offset by the visual weight of the rocks in the lower right.

- **Radial**: Radial balance (**Figure 7.45**) is a circular type of balance that radiates from the center instead of the middle of a design. Many artists get the feeling that they're viewing a radially balanced image from above. This kind of balance is almost always circular. An excellent example of radial balance is a kaleidoscopic image, which can feel balanced and unified but also typically feels more static than the other types of balance.

Figure 7.45 This image has a radial balance.

The Principle of Proportion or Scale

Proportion, sometimes called scale, describes the relative sizes and scale of things. If you've ever seen a drawing and observed that "the head is too small" or "the body is too fat," you're evaluating the proportion. It's simply the sense that things seem to be the proper size relative to each other.

▶ Video 7.19
Design School: The Principle of Proportion or Scale

You can manipulate proportion and scale to create emphasis. Things that are larger than they should be appear stronger, more important, or more powerful. Take the chapter headings in this book. By making the headings disproportionately large, we've indicated importance and emphasis. You can also reduce the perceived value, strength, or importance of something by reducing its scale.

The Principles of Repetition and Pattern

The two principles of repetition and pattern—along with movement and rhythm—seem to be the most confusing and difficult to grasp. As a matter of fact, some artists and writers more readily connect pattern and repetition with rhythm than with movement. In this introductory look at these concepts, think about the simplest and most concrete uses of them here. As always, you're encouraged to explore these areas much more deeply on your own.

▶ Video 7.20
Design School: The Principles of Repetition and Pattern

Repetition is a principle that is pretty easy to grasp: repeating an element in your design. Repetition can convey many things, but it often represents importance, movement, or energy. Think of an illustration of a ball moving or a cartoon of a bird flapping its wings. Just repeating a few lines can convey a sense of motion.

Pattern happens when different objects repeat in a sequence. The best way to think about the difference between repetition and pattern is that repetition is done with a single element (such as pinstripes on a suit), whereas pattern happens with a collection of elements (such as a floral pattern on fabric). Pattern also happens when elements are repeated consistently and, at some point, eventually move past repetition and become a pattern.

Another important way to think about repetition is to share certain traits of the elements in your design. Doing so brings some unity to those elements and lets the viewer know they're related. For example, you could repeat the colors of the logo in headers and bold type or repeat the same colors from a photo into the header text of an associated article in a magazine. Repetition of this kind conveys a sense of unity in the design.

The Principles of Movement and Rhythm

▶ *Video 7.21*
Design School:
The Principles of
Movement and
Rhythm

Movement and rhythm are similar, much like repetition and pattern. They modify an image much the way an adverb modifies an adjective. They explain a feeling that the elements create, rather than making specific changes to the elements.

Movement refers to the visual movement in an image. Depending on the context, it can refer to the movement the eye naturally follows across an image as it moves from focal point to focal point, or the perceived movement or flow of the elements in the image.

Movement can also refer to the "flow" of an image and is a critical principle to consider in your work. It's more of a feeling than a concrete visual aspect of your design. When something "doesn't feel right," it may be that the flow is uncertain or contradictory. If you haven't considered the flow of your design, analyze it and create a flow that guides the viewer through your design. The more linear your flow, the more your design will convey a sense of reliability, consistency, and calm. A more complex flow can convey a sense of creativity, freedom, or even chaos.

Rhythm refers to the visual "beat" in the design, a sense of an irregular but predictable pattern. Just as a rhythm is laid down by a drummer, a design's rhythm is creative and expressive, rather than a consistent pattern or repetition. Depending on the design you're working on, rhythm may or may not be a critical principle to consider. A predictable rhythm can convey a sense of calm and consistency, whereas an erratic or complex rhythm can convey a sense of urgency or energy.

These two principles tend to be the most subjective, so be sure to clarify anything you're unsure about when discussing these principles with a client. Because they're more of a feeling than a specific element or technique, it takes a little experience to get a handle on them. But these are just like all of the principles; once you start looking for them, you'll start to see them.

Wrapping Up the Design Concepts

As a visual designer, you must understand the elements and principles so that your work can communicate clearly to your audience. Learning the technical basics of Illustrator is fairly easy, and they can be mastered by people who will never "make it" in the industry.

▶ *Video 7.22* Design School: Wrapping Up Design School

Take the time to develop your design skills set and to remember that it *is* a skills set. You've got to practice and continue to develop your craft to level up those skills. Using Illustrator without having a design sense is like starting up a jet engine without the jet. It's powerful, but you won't be able to fly it to a destination. The artistic elements and principles are the wings and controls that let you harness that power and get your art to go where you want it.

Invest the time and effort to practice and refine your design sense. You'll find that your personal art not only grows more impressive over time but that the entire world opens up and becomes much more interesting, beautiful, and detailed.

Illustrator is about learning to create visual designs with exceptionally high quality and detail, but becoming an artist and refining your skills is about learning to *see*.

Open your eyes...and enjoy the beauty you've been missing that's all around you!

 TIP

Connect with us at www.brainbuffet.com/design to see our ever-growing collection of design-related resources or follow us on Twitter @brainbuffet for weekly resources, inspiration, and freebies to use with your design projects.

CHAPTER OBJECTIVES

Chapter Learning Objectives

- Understand your client's needs.
- Familiarize yourself with copyright and licensing basics.
- Explore project management.
- Avoid project creep.

Chapter ACA Objectives

For full descriptions of the objectives, see the table on pages 196–204.

DOMAIN 1.0
WORKING IN THE DESIGN INDUSTRY
1.1, 1.2, 1.3

CHAPTER 8

Working with Outsiders

As a visual designer, you're going to work with others. Being a designer and being an artist are two different careers, but most people who do creative work for a living find a need to do both. It's similar to the way a lot of photographers shoot weddings to pay the bills. It may not be their favorite type of photography, but it pays well and makes people happy. However, if you love to shoot old, crumbly walls and rusty farmhouse doors, you will find that you simply can't pay the bills with your "rusty hinge" photo collection.

Aside from the money, you will probably learn to develop an immense passion for creating designs for others. The secret to this part of the job is project planning twofold: really listen and really care.

▶ *Video 8.1*
Introduction to Project Planning

Who You're Talking for and Who You're Talking to

★ ACA Objective 1.1 The first step in designing for a particular project is to understand the client's needs.

This is critical because, among other things, the client pays the bills. Most of all, the client is hiring you to speak for them. As a visual designer, that's a weighty responsibility. You're being trusted to communicate for an entire company or cause. First and foremost, you need to address that client's needs and goals for the project. This will be the guiding principle when answering design questions. You must constantly remember your goals and focus narrowly on them to streamline your workflow and minimize distractions.

Let's look at a few example scenarios:

- Rockin' Zombies is a metal-opera-jazz-bluegrass fusion band that wants to promote an upcoming free concert at the local farmer's market.
- Hoi Polloi Church needs a brochure for their project to solicit volunteers and donations to help orphaned children recover from Hurricane Sally.
- OfficeHome Custodial Services wants to share information with businesses about their upscale, environmentally friendly office cleaning services.
- Zak's Bulldozer wants to promote their tree removal for residential homes using low-impact tools.
- The city's Health Department wants a campaign to promote healthy eating and active lifestyle changes and to inform and warn people about common bad habits.
- Pop-Lite is a new, collapsible photo light, and the inventors need a logo and image for their Kickstarter campaign.

Each project has different goals, right? Some want to give away something for free. Some want to make money. Some want to solicit help from others. It's important to help clients pin down their project goals—and that can be hard to do.

Single Voice, Single Message

▶ Video 8.2
Discovering Client Goals

Here's a brainteaser: You're in a room with 20 close friends, but you cannot understand what they say. Why? They are all speaking loud enough for you to hear clearly. They are all speaking your language. None of you have any health or physical impairments that affect speech or hearing. What's the problem?

They're all talking at once!

If a design says too much, it says nothing. It becomes "noisy" and makes it hard for the viewer to focus on the main idea. This reality is similar to the design concept of focal point. All creative projects have a kind of focal point. It's important to clearly define and pin down the most important goals of a project. Sometimes, clients are trying to clearly define their purpose, vision, or dreams for their organization. The overall goals and dreams for the business are helpful in the design process and should be heard so that you understand your client. But to get a project done efficiently—and create a project that communicates well—you must work with the client to establish and narrow down the goals for this project.

This short version of a campaign's goals is often called the "elevator pitch" because it summarizes the project in the time that it would take for an elevator ride. It's communicating your purpose in a short, simple sentence. Normally, I push a client to shoot for seven words or less. The aim is to clearly define the goals for this particular design project.

Here are some elevator pitches related to the scenarios listed earlier:

- Come to our free concert.
- Help child victims of a disaster.
- Get safe cleaning services for your office.
- Trees removed without damaging your yard.
- Get healthy and avoid hidden dangers.
- Our little photo lights are fun and functional.

Admittedly, these pitches are not elegant or enticing. There's no "pop" to the message. But they're the very core of what you're trying to communicate. It is the reason your client is paying you to design the project. You'll need more detail than this to deliver an effective design, but focusing on this core goal can help you rein in the insidious forces of project creep (which we'll talk about later in this chapter). But first, let this sink in: your client's goals are your number-one priority.

If the goal is unclear, the finished product will be unclear. Figure out the goal, and you can always come back to it as a "home base" when the project starts to grow or lose its focus. Sometimes the goal isn't obvious, or it turns out to be different than it first appeared. But it's always critical, and one of your first jobs is to help the client focus on the primary goal of the project. Nonetheless, at the end of the day you work for the client, so the client calls the shots, has the final say, and makes the decisions—even if you disagree.

Now we'll talk about the second-most important person on the project—the one who doesn't really exist. I'm talking about the ideal audience for the piece.

★ *ACA Objective 1.1*

 *Video 8.3*
  Finding the
  Target Audience

Identifying Your Client's Ideal Customer

In life, we shouldn't judge people, make assumptions, and lump people together.

But we do. And as creative professionals, we *must*. This means developing a demographic for the project and identifying the target audience. It's a critical step in helping your clients bridge the gap to the audience they want to reach. You do this by identifying the common characteristics of that audience and creating an image in everyone's minds of the typical customer. Some clients will say "Everybody needs my product," but those clients will still need to focus on a target demographic specific to the project at hand. As the old saying goes, "Aim at nothing and you'll hit it every time." Those are wise words, especially when identifying a target audience.

Identifying a target demographic for your project is a critical step, second only to defining the client's goals. And generally, it's also a part of the client's goals. For example, when you want to create a new fishing pole, you can easily picture your target audience: people who like to fish. So you're probably not going to use the same graphics, words, images, or feel as you would to reach a punk rock audience. At the same time, expectant mothers probably wouldn't be drawn to those images.

Identifying a demographic helps you focus on who you want to get your message. Understand the goals of your viewer as well as the speaker, your client. Make sure you share information in a way that will connect or resonate with that audience. And if you understand what your audience needs and feels, you can show how what you're sharing meets those needs.

The easiest way to do this is to create imaginary "perfect fits" for your client's project. Here are some things to consider:

- **Income:** Determine if you want to focus on quality, exclusivity, or price.
- **Education:** Establish the vocabulary and complexity of the design.
- **Age:** Dictate the general appeal, attitude, and vocabulary.
- **Hobbies:** Help in choosing images, insider vocabulary, and attitudes.
- **Concerns, cares, and passions:** Identify core beliefs, trigger points, and so on.

It's easy to see how different audiences will need different images. You don't want images of extreme sports in an ad aimed at expectant mothers. You wouldn't use a crowded nightclub image in a design for a camping and canoe outfitter company. Inexperienced designers sometimes try to make a production to please themselves, and that isn't always what pleases the target audience.

What makes your audience unique? Who has the problems that this product solves? Have those pictures in your mind. Work these ideas over with your client and help them envision their typical customer. Then look for images that will appeal to that ideal customer, this project's target demographic.

Think of yourself as a matchmaker. You're trying to introduce your client to the perfect customer or consumer. Speak in the language that the ideal customer would want to hear, and use images that will bring their lifestyle and outlook together with your client.

The Golden Rule for Client Projects

Effective design helps someone else convey his vision. It communicates a message. When you're starting a new edit, use the business version of the golden rule: he who has the gold makes the rules.

▶ **Video 8.4** *The Golden Rule for Client Work*

Ultimately, you work for your clients. Help them see what you regard as the most effective way and identify the right questions to ask, but don't fight with them. They might have insight or perspective about their target audience that you don't have. Even when you disagree with a client about a design decision, you still need to help her realize her vision for her project. If you don't like it, you don't have to put the final piece in your portfolio, but you'll still get to put her check in the bank. If it comes down to what the client wants versus what you think her audience will respond to, do what the client asks. It's her project, her audience, and her money.

There's one exception to this rule that you need to follow at all times. When your client asks you to skirt copyright law, you're still responsible for respecting the law and your fellow creative professionals. Often the clients are just confused and you can help them understand that you can't copy other designs or employ copyrighted materials without authorization. Along those lines, let's take a moment to talk about copyright.

Copyrights and Wrongs

★ *ACA Objective 1.3*

Copyright is an amazing set of laws designed to protect and promote artists along with their art, creativity, and learning. It's gotten a bad rap, and you can set aside any preconceived ideas for a bit and think through the copyright concept (**Figure 8.1**).

Figure 8.1 Copyright can be a complex issue, but the basics are straightforward.

Copyright law is generally misunderstood by the public, so understanding it is an awesome way to score high at trivia night. A solid understanding of copyright law will also enable you to help your struggling author and artist friends realize that they don't have to pay an attorney tons of money to "make sure they get their stuff copyrighted." You can do it for them or show them how to do it themselves. It's free and easy. As a matter of fact, it's probably already been done.

Keep in mind that I'm a designer and instructor, not a lawyer. This chapter does not constitute legal advice; it's just intended to help you understand the law and the reasons it exists so you can appreciate it. It's easier to obey a law that you understand and appreciate, and copyright laws protect your rights. So get on board.

Here's something to remember: Copyright law promotes freedom and creativity. Let's explore how.

Copyright Happens

The first thing to know about copyright in the United States is that it just happens. If something can be copied, then it's copyrighted. You needn't fill out any special forms, report to a government office, or do anything extra to put it in place. The law is written so that copyright happens as soon as something original and creative is recorded in a "fixed form." This means that as soon as you write something down, sketch it out, or click the shutter on your camera, whatever you just created is copyrighted. The only reason you might do anything additional is to establish verifiable proof of when a creation was copyrighted, because the person who can prove that she recorded it first owns the copyright.

▶ *Video 8.5* *About Copyright*

Imagine that you're in a restaurant talking with a friend. During this conversation you make up a song on the spot. A famous singer in the booth behind yours hears you and writes it down. He claims the copyright to the lyrics and melody and makes a million bucks with your spontaneous song, and there's little you can do about it. However, if you recorded it on your phone when you sang it, you recorded it in fixed form *first*. So, *you* own the copyright on the lyrics, and the artist now owes you a truckload of money.

Why does the law have this quirky little rule? Because the courts have to decide who owns copyright when its ownership is contested in court. And courts rely on tangible proof. So the law makes it simple by stating that she who first records something in fixed form wins. This way, you're not going to sue someone if you have no proof that you were first. But even if you were and you can't prove it, you're out of luck.

So why do we have a copyright notice on music, DVDs, and one of the first pages of this book? If we don't need it, why do we display it?

Simply put, it reminds people who owns this copyrighted material. When no date and copyright symbol are displayed, people may think they can legally make photocopies of this book for their friends. Most people assume if no copyright notice appears, then no copyright exists. (They're totally wrong.) The presence of a visible copyright statement discourages this conclusion and behavior.

So it certainly can't cause any harm to scratch a copyright symbol on your art when you're done with it, but it's more to remind *the public* than to protect *you*. You're already protected by law. Adding the copyright symbol to your work is like putting one of those security system signs in your front yard. It won't stop a determined

TIP

Although your original work is automatically copyrighted without registering it with the U.S. Copyright Office, you can potentially collect much higher monetary damages from an infringer if you do register the work.

thief, but it can deter less committed offenders. Still, if you think it makes your front yard look cheap, you don't need it for protection. The system already protects you.

Placing a Copyright Notice in Digital Content

Video 8.6 *Digital Tools for Tracking Copyright*

The beauty of digital files is that they have the ability to contain hidden information that never compromises the enjoyment of the document itself. As a result, you can add copyright information to digital content without having a visually distracting copyright notice on the artwork (**Figure 8.2**). You do this by adding information called metadata into your digital files.

Metadata is information that doesn't show up on the document itself but is hidden inside the file. This is a perfect way to store copyright information, contact details, and so on. On some digital cameras, metadata can record the lens information, the location via GPS, whether a flash was attached and fired, the camera settings, and more. In digital files, metadata can share the computer on which it was created, the time, and the name of the creator. (This is how good technology teachers catch cheaters.) Be sure to make use of metadata when you're sending your work out over the web, and always check files that your clients give you to make sure that you're not violating another professional's means of making money when you're trying to make some yourself.

Figure 8.2 You don't need the mark or any sort of label, but it does make sure others know your work is copyrighted.

"But I'm not trying to make any money with their art, so it's okay, right?" Well, that's a tough question with a few interesting rules attached.

★ *ACA Objective 1.3*

 **Video 8.7** *Fair Use and Copyright*

Playing Fair with Copyrighted Material

Can you use copyrighted material when you're practicing with Illustrator CC? Can you make a funny image using a movie poster by replacing the faces of the actors with the faces of your friends? What about using cool logos from your favorite companies as you're learning Illustrator CC?

These uses of copyrighted material are completely legit. The people who came up with our copyright laws were careful to make sure that the laws don't limit—but instead promote—creativity. They did this with a set of ideas called fair use.

Fair use policy is a set of rules that make sure copyright protection doesn't come at the cost of creativity and freedom. Copyright can't be used to limit someone's personal growth or learning, freedom of speech, or artistic expression and creative exploration. Those ideas are more important than copyright, so copyright doesn't apply when it gets in the way of these higher ideals. You're free to use copyrighted materials in the pursuit of these higher goals. Some people (mistakenly) believe that fair use doesn't apply to copyrighted materials, but in fact, it applies only to copyrighted materials. Here is a list of issues that a court would consider when making a decision about fair use:

- **Purpose: If you use the work to teach, learn, voice your own opinion, inspire you to create a new piece of art, or report news, you're probably safe.** Protected reasons include educational purposes (teaching, research), freedom of speech (commentary or criticism), news reporting, and transformative work (parody or using the work in a new way). It isn't considered fair use if you're making money from the use, using it just for entertainment, or trying to pass it off as your own work.

- **Nature: If the nature of the original work is factual, the work is published information, or the work is critical to favoring education, you're probably safe.** Was the content already published, fact based, and important for society to know? Then you're pretty safe to use the work. But if it was unpublished, creative (such as art, music, film, novels), and fictional, you're probably not cleared to use it.

- **Amount: If you use a small amount of a copyrighted work, it's more likely that your use of the work is fair use.** If you use only a small quantity—not the main idea or focus of the work, but just enough to teach or learn from— you're probably safe. If you use a large portion of the work or basically rip off the central idea, or the "heart of the work," it isn't fair use.

- **Effect: If nobody is harmed because of the action you've taken, then your action is probably fair use.** If you use a legitimate copy of the original work, it doesn't affect the sale of another copy, and you have no other way to get a copy, you're in pretty good shape. But if your copy makes it less likely that someone would buy a copy or you made a large number of copies, you're probably hurting the original creator, and that's not fair use.

As mentioned earlier, copyright law addresses a simple question: "How can we promote more freedom and creativity in the world?" This is the question that copyright laws seek to answer. Fair use makes sure that beginning artists can experiment using anything they want. Just be sure not to share anything that might be another artist's copyrighted work.

But as a beginning designer, how can you get good-quality assets to use in real-world projects? Happily, you have access to more free resources than ever before in history via the Internet and free stock photos. We'll look at some in the next section.

Uncopyrighting

▶ **Video 8.8**
Licensing: Strict and Free

You have a couple of ways in which to undo copyright. One is voluntary. An author can choose to release the copyright to his material. Believe it or not, this can be more difficult to do than you'd expect. Copyright law protects creators of their works, and it can be difficult to *not* be protected by copyright law.

The second way is to let the copyright expire. Copyrights normally expire between 50 and 100 years after the death of the original author, but exceptions to this rule exist, and extensions can be requested. It's beyond the scope of this book to discuss copyright at length, but it's important to realize that some materials have expired copyrights. When copyright is expired or released, the work is said to be in the public domain. This means that copyright no longer applies to the content, and you can use the material without worrying about copyright infringement.

Licensing

★ *ACA Objective 1.3*

Licensing is another way that you can legally use copyrighted material. For designers and artists, licensing is fairly common because it allows us to use copyrighted material for a certain time and in a certain way by paying a fee established by the copyright holder according to the use of the material.

Stock photos are popular items licensed by all sorts of designers, and you can find them from many sources at various prices. Stock photos are images for which the author retains copyright but you can purchase a license to use these images in your designs. For almost everyone, this is a much less expensive solution than hiring a photographer to go to a location and shoot, process, and sell you the rights to an image.

CREATIVE COMMONS

In the last decade or so, a lot of exploration has been done in finding alternative ways to license creative works. Creative Commons licensing (**Figure 8.3**) is built on copyright law but offers ways that artists can release their works for limited use and still choose the way the works are used and shared.

Creative Commons licenses include many different combinations of the following attributes, so you'll need to do some research when using Creative Commons licensed materials and when releasing assets with Creative Commons licensing.

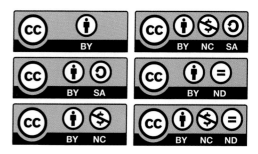

Figure 8.3 Creative Commons licenses allow for a variety of easy-to-understand licensing options.

- **Public Domain** (CC0) licenses allow artists to release their works to the public domain. It's a bit difficult to give your materials away to the public domain, but CC0 is generally recognized as a way to do so and is respected in most parts of the world.

- **Attribution** (BY) requires that you credit the original author when using her work. You can do whatever you want with the work as long as you give that credit.

- **ShareAlike** (SA) allows you to use the item in anything you want as long as your creation is shared under the same license as the original work.

- **NoDerivs** (ND) requires that you not change the material when you incorporate it into your own work. You can use NoDerivs material freely, but you must pass it along without changing it.

- **NonCommercial** (NC) means that people can use your work in their own creative works as long as they don't charge for it. You're getting it for free, so if you want to use it, then you have to be generous and also give away your work for free.

Creative Commons licenses are widely accepted and used, and you can find a ton of amazing resources that use this licensing. If you have any questions about Creative Commons licenses, you can find out everything from a general overview to detailed legal descriptions at *www.creativecommons.org*.

PEOPLE PERMISSIONS

Because some assets we use in Illustrator include photographs, we need to talk about extra permissions such as model releases. This type of release is required when a person's face is identifiable in the design that will be used to promote something, whether it's a product or an idea. Any work you do for a client is by definition a commercial use and will require a model release for every identifiable face.

★ *ACA Objective 1.3*

Think Like a Boss

Some might say that the only thing you need to know to succeed in life is how to solve a problem. That's not how to solve a specific problem; that would be only an exercise in memory. A well-trained monkey can mimic a person's actions and get a similar result. But a monkey can't think with the depth of a human. My preferred way to solve problems is to work to understand things deeply and explore all the nuances of a potential solution. But for others, this process is a little outside their comfort zones and they find it faster and easier to copy someone else's solution.

In Illustrator, copying another solution or technique means following tutorials. In entry-level jobs, it's being a dutiful employee, efficient worker, and good follower who shows up on time.

But what do you do when you're the leader? What happens when you need to do something new and fresh for your job? What if the boss doesn't know how to do it and that's why she hired you? At times, your client's main request will be something as vague and daunting as "Do something that hasn't been done before."

That's where the problem-solving process comes in—the only skill you need to be successful. If you can do that, you can figure out anything.

★ *ACA Objective 1.2*

▶ *Video 8.9* *Project Management Intro*

Project Management

Project management is just the problem-solving process in action—geared toward supervising resources, people, and team-based projects. The DNA of project management is problem solving and organizing the process so that you tackle the right issues at the right time using the right tools. Project-management systems take on many forms (as do problem-solving systems), but if you truly grasp the ideas behind the labels, you can translate them into whatever management strategy your client, team, or boss is using.

The problem-solving process is creative in itself. A good solution to a problem can be artistic in its elegance and efficient grace. If you can grasp problem solving, you can learn whatever you need to learn now and in the future.

The following procedure will help when you need to solve a technical problem on hardware or equipment, handle an editing issue within your visual design project, or figure out how to get your hand out of that jar you got it stuck in. It will help you translate a tutorial written for Illustrator CS6 into your current version (things change fast these days!). And it boils down to three simple steps: learn, think, and do.

Learn

The first step of a problem-solving process is to learn. It includes two important steps: learning what the problem is and learning how others have solved similar problems (research and investigate). It seems simple, but the process can be confusing. Most projects with major problems get stuck at this initial step because they didn't learn well—or at all. Let's talk about them.

UNDERSTAND THE PROBLEM

As we discussed earlier in this chapter, the first step of every project is to understand the problem. For most design projects, you must figure out how to most effectively help your client share his goals with the target audience. If the client is yourself, then it's about getting to the essence of what you want to communicate and communicating it so that your target audience can act on it.

▶ *Video 8.10*
Project Management—Understand the Problem

Understanding the problem is the most difficult part of the problem-solving process. Mess it up here, and by definition, you're not solving the problem. You haven't properly identified the problem, so how can you solve it? Sometimes you can make the problem worse by implementing a plan that creates a new problem without solving the real one.

You can avoid trouble down the road by clearly understanding and defining the problem at the start. "I want to sell a million widgets" is not a problem you can solve; it's a desire the client has. So what's the problem you can help with? He hasn't sold as many as he wants? That's not it either. How do you get to the bottom of the problem?

Start with good questions: Do people need a widget? If so, do people know widgets are a thing? If so, do they choose a competing widget? If so, why do they choose this other widget? Why do you think they should use your widget instead? Who would be most likely to buy your widget? What is your budget for widget advertising? What do you want to spend on this particular project? What are your expectations?

Many clients become frustrated with this set of questions. They just want action to be taken so that they can feel like they're doing something. But let me repeat that old saying: "Aim at nothing, and you'll hit it every time." This is when you sharpen your axe so you don't have to chop at the tree all day.

This part of the project can be fairly informal on smaller projects but can be huge on large projects. Here's a list of critical questions to answer:

- **Purpose:** Why are you doing this creative project? What result would you consider a success?
- **Target:** Who needs this message or product? Describe your typical customer.
- **Limits:** What are the limits for the project? Budget and time are most necessary to nail down.
- **Preferences:** Aside from the results we've already discussed, are there any other results you'd like or expect from this project?

These examples are intended to show how quickly you can determine a client's expectations. The answers to these questions define the size of the job and how you'll best be able to work with the client.

Sketches and written notes from this initial step will help. Gather as much information as you can to make the rest of the project go smoothly. The more you find out now, the less you'll have to redesign later, because the client hates the color, the layout, or the general direction you took the project. Invest the time now, or pay it back with interest later. With a clear idea of what the problem is, you'll get the information you need to solve it in the next step.

RESEARCH AND INVESTIGATE

After you understand exactly what your client is expecting, you can start doing the research to arrive at the answers you need. Let's take a quick look at that word: *re-search*. It literally means "search again." Lots of people fail to research; they just search. They look at the most obvious places and approaches, and if things don't immediately click, they settle for a poor but quick and easy solution.

Depending on the job, researching can be a relatively quick process. Find out about the competitive products, learn about the problem you're trying to solve, and understand the demographic you're going to target. The more research you do, the better information you'll have about the problem you're trying to solve, which will help you with the next step.

Think

The next couple of steps represent the "thinking" phase. You can do this quickly using a pen and a napkin, or you can do it in depth and generate tons of documentation along the way, particularly on large projects (**Figure 8.4**). But thinking is the part that most of us often mistake as the beginning. Remember that if the learning step isn't done well, your thinking step might be headed in the wrong direction.

▶ *Video 8.11*
Project Management— Think It Through

Figure 8.4 As a designer, you'll often do much of your thinking on paper, even if you're not producing traditional or formal storyboards. Sketch out your sequence first and have that reference to show the customer and to come back to for clarity.

BRAINSTORM

The next step is to brainstorm. As with research, you need to grasp the meaning. It's a brain**storm**. Not a brain *drizzle*. A full-on typhoon of ideas. At this point, it's important to stop thinking analytically and start thinking creatively. If you start thinking critically instead of creatively, you'll change direction and you'll lose ground on your brainstorming task. If you start moving in the critical direction, that's the opposite of creative. Stop that! Don't try to work hard on brainstorming. Work relaxed instead.

At times, analysis will need to happen. You start analyzing how to complete your ideas when you should be creating them. Here are some things *not* to do when brainstorming, including trains of thought that can trigger critical modes of thinking:

CRITICAL THOUGHTS	CREATIVE THINGS
Judging your ideas	Listen to music.
Trying to finish an idea when you should still be brainstorming	Look at cool art online.
	Call a friend.
Getting stuck on a particular idea	Doodle on something.
Planning out the project	Read a poem.
Thinking about how much time you have	Take a break.
Thinking about the budget	Go for a walk.
Thinking about numbers	Watch a movie.
Grouping or sorting your ideas	Write a haiku.
Developing the idea that you think is best	Meditate for five minutes.
	Exercise.
	Sleep on it.

When you're in brainstorming mode, don't edit your ideas. Let them flow. If a crummy idea pops into your head, put it on paper. If you don't, it will keep popping up until it's been given a little respect. Give the weak ideas respect; they open doors for the great ones. Brainstorming is a matter of quantity, not quality.

PICK AND PLAN

► *Video 8.12*
Project Management— Get It in Writing

After brainstorming, you need to pick a solution that you generated in your brainstorming session and plan things out. You'll find that the plan you go with is rarely your first idea. Through the process of brainstorming, the idea will go through several iterations. A common mistake for beginners is to fall in love with an early idea—beware of this pitfall! Your best idea is lurking in the background of your mind, and you have to get rid of all the simple ideas that pop up first. For a small project or a one-person team, you might quickly hammer out a contract and get to work, but in larger projects, the planning needs to be detailed and focused.

The larger the project, the more formal this process will be. Small projects with just one person working on it will have little planning necessary for moving forward. However, larger projects will need a project plan to set the project requirements for the team.

SETTING PROJECT REQUIREMENTS

This is where the action happens. Look through the ideas you've generated and pick the one that seems best and plan how to make it happen. This is where you determine exactly what has to be done, establish some direction, and identify a clear target. This planning stage (which most creative types naturally tend to resist, myself included) is where you clarify what needs to be done; it establishes your direction and identifies a clear target. We resist it because it seems to limit us. It ropes in our creative freedom, and it gives us a checklist—all things that many creatives hate. These things are creative kryptonite—or at least we *think* they are. But let's consider this for a moment.

★ *ACA Objective 1.2*

If you don't perform this admittedly tedious step, what won't you have? You won't have a definition of what needs to be done, a direction to head in, or a target to hit. Everyone will be in the dark. Although this step doesn't seem creative in itself, creativity isn't the priority at this particular juncture. You're at a journey-versus-destination moment. Creativity without limits is a journey, which is great for your own work but a disaster for a client-driven job. A client-driven project requires clearly defined goals—a destination. You need to arrive somewhere specific.

Two critical points that must be a part of every project plan are the project scope and the project deadline. Every contract needs to have these critical components defined to focus the project:

★ *ACA Objective 1.2*

- **Project scope** is the amount of work to be done. On the designer's side, this is the most important thing to establish. If the scope isn't clear, you're subject to the Achilles heel of editing and production work: **project creep**. This is a pervasive problem in our industry (you'll learn more later in this chapter), but simply writing down a defined scope can prevent the problem. Get in writing *exactly* what you need to do and make sure specific numbers are attached.

- **Project deadlines** dictate when the work needs to be done. This is the client's most important element. The deadline often affects the price. If the client needs 10 animated banner ads in six months, you can probably offer a discount. If they need a draft by tomorrow morning, then they'll have to pay an additional "rush" fee. Deadlines on large projects also can be broken down into phases, each with its own fee. This division of tasks helps you pay the bills by generating cash flow during a large and lengthy project. It also limits the impact—for you—of payment delay.

I strongly encourage you to include the following additional items in your creative project plans. These items, when shared and discussed with your client, will save time, money, and disagreements. These additional deliverables are the raw materials of project planning and help convey the exact target of the project. The following two deliverables are critical for every production project:

- Sketches are helpful to show the client how your project and edit will flow. It's even better when the client has an idea of what they're looking for and can give you their own storyboard, however crude. Does this limit your creative freedom? Yes, and it also saves you a ton of time. The goal of a client job is to get a project done to his satisfaction. If the client is particular and knows what he wants, you're not going to convince him otherwise. Sketches save time because they limit your direction to one that the client will accept, and they help you get to that acceptance faster. That means you get finished and paid sooner. The better the storyboards are before you get into actual editing, the fewer changes and revisions you'll need. You don't have to be a master sketch artist; just convey the idea. Sometimes sketches may just be wireframes—very rough representative sketches of how to lay out the project—especially in regard to interactive media projects.

- Specifications, or specs, are detailed, clearly written goals and limits for a project. Many times, the specifications themselves will be referred to as the "project plan" and become part of the contract. This will involve the target platform and feature set of the interactive project. All project plans should include two critical pieces of information: the scope of the project and the deadlines that need to be met. Be sure to always include both of these items in your project specifications.

⭐ *ACA Objective 1.2*

▶ *Video 8.13*
*Project
Management—
Avoiding Creep*

AVOIDING PROJECT CREEP

Project creep occurs when a project starts to lose its focus and spin out of control, eating up more and more time and effort. It is important to be aware of this phenomenon. It happens all the time, and the main culprit in every case is a poorly designed project plan that lacks clear specifications and deadlines.

Here's how it happens: Joe Client creates a product and wants to sell it. He comes to you for marketing materials. You determine that he wants a logo, a flyer, and a three-page informational website. You've settled on a price of $4,500 and you've got a month to get it done. You go to work.

Then Joe realizes that he also wants some images for social media. Could you just make a few? He also realizes that he needs to put his new logo on new business cards. Could you just design a card with the logo on it? Oh, and he can't figure out how to get his product onto his favorite online marketplace. Could you just help him set that up? And he changed his launch date. He doesn't need it next month, he needs it next week because he just reserved a booth at a large convention. By the way, do you know anything about designing booths?

This is why it's critical to create a detailed project plan with task definitions and deadlines attached. Sometimes the client asks for something and it takes you 30 seconds. It's a good idea to always happily deliver on these little items. A favor is any job that takes you five minutes or less. After that, the favor turns into work. And your only defense is your contract defining a *clearly stated* scope.

Just make sure that the project's scope is clearly stated. If the contract says that you'll provide *any* images for the company's web presence, you're in trouble. If it says that you'll specifically provide up to nine images for the client's website, you're in great shape. Taking the hour it requires to specify your project and its deadlines in detail will save you from many hours of work and contract revisions.

If the client has approved your project parameters and then asks for something different, you need to charge him for the change if it's going to take more than 5 to 10 minutes. Sticking to this policy helps the client think about changes before sending them to you. If you fail to charge when addressing impromptu changes, the client has no reason to think about the requests in advance. Charging customers for additional changes focuses them on what they really want.

Of course, if the client asks for something that makes the job easier and faster, then make the change and do it for free. The bottom line is this: establish goodwill whenever it's good for both you and your client. But when an 11th-hour alteration serves only one side of the relationship, the requesting side has to pay for the service. This arrangement ensures that everyone ends up winning.

Do

The last phase of the project plan is to knock it out! This is the "two snaps and a twist" phase because it generally happens quickly when you have a good plan—unless there's a hitch. But at this point, on most design projects you're pretty much wrapping things up.

▶ *Video 8.14*
Project Management—Make It So

BUILD IT

This step is obvious: make it happen. This phase is where most people think all the action is...but honestly, if you've done the prior steps well, this can be the fastest part of the process. You already know what to do—now just do it. The design decisions and feature specifications have been made and you can get to work. Of course, when doing this step, regularly refer to the specifications and keep the client informed. The best way to do so is to have a feedback loop in place.

FEEDBACK LOOP

★ *ACA Objective 1.2*

A feedback loop is a system set up to constantly encourage and require input and approvals on the project direction. Keeping your client informed is the best way to speed through the process. For an interactive media project, iterative work establishes effective guideposts to send to the client for review and input. Iterative work is work you're sharing as it's done. Doing so performs a couple of critical functions. First, it lets the client see that work's being done and helps reassure her that the process has momentum. Second, it lets the client chime in on anything that she doesn't like while it's still easy to make a change.

Using Creative Cloud files is a great way to share iterative work with a client while allowing them to comment on a project throughout the process. Establishing this open communications channel encourages and enforces a healthy exchange of opinions and can enable you to most efficiently adjust and fine-tune your project to suit your client.

TEST AND EVALUATE

This very last step can also be fast if you've had a good feedback loop in place. For visual design projects, it's essentially checking the work against your project plan and making sure that you met all the specifications to satisfy you and your client. If not, you should essentially start the problem-solving process again to understand the current problem. Find out exactly what the client believes doesn't meet the requirements.

Assuming a good project plan with storyboards and a good feedback loop, the test-and-evaluation phase should require only minor tweaks—no different from any other iterative work resolution. If you don't have a good feedback loop and the first time the client sees your work is upon delivery, that client could become unhappy and demand innumerable changes. Avoid this migraine with an effective and well-defined feedback loop as part of your plan. Those two tools are your weapons against project creep and unreasonable clients.

WORKING FOR "THE MAN"

Many visual designers begin their careers working at larger firms, which can be a much easier way to get started than freelancing with your own business. If you're exclusively an artist, this type of job may require you only to do the tasks you're best at doing. In a large firm, someone else does the sales, manages client relationships and projects, and creates technical specifications.

As an artist at a larger firm, you're responsible only for working with footage and editing it. Everything else is handled by someone else, which is a good trade-off for artists who don't like the detail-oriented checklist work of project management and bookkeeping.

Working within an experienced company can also be an amazing education. You can develop your strengths, learn about the industry, and slowly increase your involvement in the other aspects of this career beyond Illustrator proficiency.

▶ **Video 8.15** *The Advantages of Working at a Firm*

Conclusion

Much of this chapter digressed from the hands-on Illustrator work that similar books cover. But starting their careers without the information presented in this chapter can pose a problem for many beginning artists. You need to master a lot of industry information, creative knowledge, and business skills to be successful. We're stoked that you read this far. Many of us creative people have a hard time with the business side of the career, but it's best to understand these ideas and concepts now before a lack of understanding becomes a problem. The tips and techniques that you've read in this chapter will eliminate a lot of the inherent frustration in the complexity of working with and for other people.

Illustrator is an intensely creative and varied application that tends to attract adventurous individuals. The qualities that make us great at thinking outside the box and designing new and beautiful images are the same qualities that may make us less skilled at the organized detail work of business and client management.

▶ **Video 8.16** *Wrapping Up Project Planning*

ACA Objectives Covered

DOMAIN OBJECTIVES	CHAPTER	VIDEO
DOMAIN 1.0 Working in the Design Industry		
1.1 Identify the purpose, audience, and audience needs for preparing images.	**Ch 1** Creating a New Document, 10 **Ch 8** Who You're Talking for and Who You're Talking to, 176	**8.2** Discovering Client Goals **8.3** Finding the Target Audience
1.2 Communicate with colleagues and clients about design plans.	**Ch 8** Project Management, 186 **Ch 8** Setting Project Requirements, 191 **Ch 8** Project Scope, 191 **Ch 8** Avoiding Project Creep, 192 **Ch 8** Feedback Loop, 194	**8.4** The Golden Rule for Client Work **8.9** Project Management Intro **8.10** Project Management—Understand the Problem **8.13** Project Management—Avoiding Creep **8.14** Project Management—Make It So
1.3 Determine the type of copyright, permissions, and licensing required to use specific content.	**Ch 8** Copyrights and Wrongs, 180 **Ch 8** Playing Fair with Copyrighted Material, 182 **Ch 8** Licensing, 184 **Ch 8** People Permissions, 185	**8.5** About Copyright **8.6** Digital Tools for Tracking Copyright **8.7** Fair Use and Copyright **8.8** Licensing: Strict and Free
1.4 Demonstrate an understanding of key terminology related to digital images.	**Ch 1** What Is Adobe Illustrator CC?, 5	**1.1** What Is Adobe Illustrator CC? **2.1** Create a New Illustrator Document
1.4a Demonstrate knowledge of digital image terminology.	**Ch 1** What Is Adobe Illustrator CC?, 5	**1.1** What Is Adobe Illustrator CC?
1.4b Demonstrate knowledge of how color is created in digital images.	**Ch 1** Customizing Document Settings, 11	
1.5 Demonstrate knowledge of basic design principles and best practices employed in the design industry.	**Ch 7** Leveling Up with Design, 131	**7.1** Design School: Introduction
1.5a Communicate visually using the elements and principles of design and common design techniques	**Ch 7** The Design Hierarchy, 133 **Ch 7** The Elements of Art, 138 **Ch 7** The Principles of Design, 165	**7.3** Design School: The Design Hierarchy **7.4** Design School: The Elements of Art **7.13** Design School: The Principles of Design

DOMAIN OBJECTIVES	CHAPTER	VIDEO
1.5b Identify and use common typographic adjustments to create contrast, hierarchy, and enhanced readability.	**Ch 7** The Element of Type, 157	**7.12** Design School: The Element of Type
1.5c Define common photographic/cinematic composition terms and principles.	**Ch 7** Applying the Design Hierarchy, 134 **Ch 7** The Element of Space, 139	**7.5** The Element of Space
DOMAIN 2.0 Project Setup and Interface		
2.1 Create a new document with the appropriate settings for web, print, and video.	**Ch 1** Creating a New Document, 10	**1.2** An Overview of the Adobe Illustrator CC Interface
2.1a Set appropriate document settings for printed and onscreen images.	**Ch 2** Creating a New Document, 27 **Ch 6** Creating a Document for a Mobile Device, 115	**2.1** Create a New Illustrator Document **6.1** Creating an Illustrator File at the Size of a Mobile Screen
2.2 Navigate, organize, and customize the application workspace.	**Ch 1** Customizing the Workspace, 14 **Ch 2** Defining Preferences in Adobe Illustrator CC, 30	
2.2a Identify and manipulate elements of the Illustrator interface.	**Ch 3** Modifying an Artboard, 47	**1.2** An Overview of the Adobe Illustrator CC Interface **3.1** Modifying Artboards
2.2b Organize and customize the workspace.		**1.3** Customizing the Workspace
2.2c Configure application preferences.		**1.2** An Overview of the Adobe Illustrator CC Interface **2.2** Defining Preferences in Adobe Illustrator CC
2.3 Use non-printing design tools in the interface to aid in project workflow.	**Ch 2** Adding Guides to the Postcard for Easy Alignment of Objects, 32	
2.3a Navigate a document	**Ch 2** Navigating a Document Effectively in Illustrator, 37 **Ch 3** Modifying an Artboard, 47	**2.6** Navigating an Illustrator Document Using Various Techniques **3.1** Modifying Artboards

continues on next page

continued from previous page

DOMAIN OBJECTIVES	CHAPTER	VIDEO
2.3b Use rulers.		**2.3** Adding Guides to a Document
2.3c Use guides and grids.	**Ch 2** Adding and Formatting Text, 40 **Ch 3** Creating a Half-Pipe for the Background of the Card, 50 **Ch 5** Adding the Frets and Fret Markers to the Neck of the Guitar, 94	**2.3** Adding Guides to a Document **2.7** Using the Type Tool to Add Text Elements to the Postcard **3.2** Creating a Half-Pipe for the Business Card **5.3** Drawing the Frets and Fret Markers on the Guitar
2.3d Use views and modes to work efficiently with vector graphics.	**Ch 3** Creating a Half-Pipe for the Background of the Card, 50 **Ch 4** Selecting Objects and Working with Groups, 67	**3.2** Creating a Half-Pipe for the Business Card **4.2** Selecting Based on Appearance and Working with Groups **5.6** Running Image Trace on an Image
2.4 Import assets into a project.	**Ch 6** Adding Text and Photos, 122	**5.1** Creating the Poster and Placing an Image **6.3** Adding Text and Images to the Mobile Mockup
2.4a Open or import images into Illustrator.	**Ch 5** Placing an Image in Adobe Illustrator, 89	**5.1** Creating the Poster and Placing an Image
2.4b Place assets in an Illustrator document.	**Ch 5** Placing an Image in Adobe Illustrator, 89 **Ch 5** Using Image Trace to Create Distressed Text, 103	**5.1** Creating the Poster and Placing an Image **5.6** Running Image Trace on an Image **5.9** Placing Text from an External File
2.5 Manage colors, swatches, and gradients.	**Ch 4** Adding a Gradient Effect and Details to the Landmarks, 81	**4.7** Adding a Gradient Effect to the Landmarks
2.5a Set the active fill and stroke color.	**Ch 2** Creating Shapes for the Postcard Background, 34 **Ch 3** Creating a Half-Pipe for the Background of the Card, 50 **Ch 3** Creating Swatches, 54 **Ch 4** Adding a Gradient Effect and Details to the Landmarks, 81	**2.4** Creating Shapes for the Background of the Postcard Project **3.2** Creating a Half-Pipe for the Business Card **3.4** Creating Swatches for the Front of the Business Card **4.7** Adding a Gradient Effect to the Landmarks
2.5b Create and/or customize a gradient.	**Ch 4** Adding a Gradient Effect and Details to the Landmarks, 81	**4.7** Adding a Gradient Effect to the Landmarks

DOMAIN OBJECTIVES	CHAPTER	VIDEO
2.5c Create, manage, and edit swatches and swatch libraries.	**Ch 3** Creating a Half-Pipe for the Background of the Card, 50 **Ch 3** Creating Swatches, 54 **Ch 4** Creating and Applying a Pattern Swatch, 79 **Ch 4** Adding a Gradient Effect and Details to the Landmarks, 81	**3.2** Creating a Half-Pipe for the Business Card **3.4** Creating Swatches for the Front of the Business Card **4.6** Creating a pattern swatch for the landmarks **4.7** Adding a Gradient Effect to the Landmarks
2.5d Use the Color Guide panel to select coordinated colors.	**Ch 3** Creating Swatches, 54	**3.4** Creating Swatches for the Front of the Business Card
2.6 Manage brushes, symbols, styles, and patterns.	**Ch 4** Finishing Up: Adding Symbols and Trimming the Artwork, 83 **Ch 5** Drawing the Bridge and Strings of the Guitar, 96 **Ch 5** Creating and Applying a Brush, 99	**4.8** Adding the Finishing Touches to the Map on the Back of the Business Card **5.4** Adding the Bridge Details and Strings **5.5** Loading, Creating, and Applying Brushes
2.6a Open and browse libraries for included brushes, symbols, graphic styles, and patterns.	**Ch 4** Using the Appearance Panel, 70 **Ch 4** Creating and Applying a Pattern Swatch, 79 **Ch 4** Finishing Up: Adding Symbols and Trimming the Artwork, 83	**4.3** Using the Appearance Panel to Add an Appearance to the Streets **4.6** Creating a Pattern Swatch for the Landmarks **4.8** Adding the Finishing Touches to the Map on the Back of the Business Card
2.6b Create and edit brushes, symbols, styles, and patterns.	**Ch 2** Drawing the Basic Lemon Artwork, 42 **Ch 4** Using the Appearance Panel, 70 **Ch 4** Creating and Applying a Pattern Swatch, 79 **Ch 4** Finishing Up: Adding Symbols and Trimming the Artwork, 83	**2.8** Drawing a Lemon Using Basic Shape Tools in Adobe Illustrator CC **4.3** Using the Appearance Panel to Add an Appearance to the Streets **4.6** Creating a Pattern Swatch for the Landmarks **4.8** Adding the Finishing Touches to the Map on the Back of the Business Card **5.5** Loading, Creating, and Applying Brushes
DOMAIN 3.0 Organization of Documents		
3.1 Use layers to manage design elements.	**Ch 4** Working with Layers, 73 **Ch 5** Drawing the Body of the Guitar, 91 **Ch 6** Adding Text and Photos, 122	**4.4** Organizing the Content on the Back of the Card Using Layers **6.3** Adding Text and Images to the Mobile Mockup

continues on next page

continued from previous page

DOMAIN OBJECTIVES	CHAPTER	VIDEO
3.1a Use the Layers panel to modify layers.	**Ch 4** Working with Layers, 73 **Ch 5** Adding the Frets and Fret Markers to the Neck of the Guitar, 94 **Ch 5** Drawing the Bridge and Strings of the Guitar, 96	**4.4** Organizing the Content on the Back of the Card Using Layers **5.3** Drawing the Frets and Fret Markers on the Guitar **5.4** Adding the Bridge Details and Strings **6.3** Adding Text and Images to the Mobile Mockup
3.1b Manage multiple layers in a complex project.	**Ch 4** Working with Layers, 73 **Ch 5** Adding the Frets and Fret Markers to the Neck of the Guitar, 94 **Ch 5** Drawing the Bridge and Strings of the Guitar, 96 **Ch 5** Adding Effects to the Music Poster, 109	**4.4** Organizing the Content on the Back of the Card Using Layers **5.3** Drawing the Frets and Fret Markers on the Guitar **5.4** Adding the Bridge Details and Strings **5.8** Adding Effects to the Music Poster
3.2 Modify layer visibility using opacity and masks.	**Ch 4** Adding a Gradient Effect and Details to the Landmarks, 81	
3.2a Adjust a layer's opacity.	**Ch 5** Adding Effects to the Music Poster, 109	**5.8** Adding Effects to the Music Poster
3.2b Create, apply, and manipulate clipping masks	**Ch 4** Finishing Up: Adding Symbols and Trimming the Artwork, 83 **Ch 5** Using Image Trace to Create Distressed Text, 103	**4.8** Adding the Finishing Touches to the Map on the Back of the Business Card

DOMAIN 4.0 Create and Modify Visual Elements

4.1 Use core tools and features to create visual elements.	**Ch 6** Creating Web Graphics Using Save For Web, 124	**2.5** Changing the Corner Appearance of an Object for the Postcard
4.1a Create images using a variety of tools.	**Ch 2** Drawing the Basic Lemon Artwork, 42 **Ch 4** Adding a Gradient Effect and Details to the Landmarks, 81 **Ch 5** Drawing the Bridge and Strings of the Guitar, 96 **Ch 5** Creating and Applying a Brush, 99 **Ch 6** Creating the Icons for the Mobile Mockup, 117	**2.8** Drawing a Lemon Using Basic Shape Tools in Adobe Illustrator CC **4.7** Adding a Gradient Effect to the Landmarks **5.4** Adding the Bridge Details and Strings **5.5** Loading, Creating, and Applying Brushes **6.2** Creating the Icons for the Mobile Mockup

DOMAIN OBJECTIVES	CHAPTER	VIDEO
4.1b Modify and edit vector images using a variety of vector tools.	**Ch 4** Drawing the Streets of the Map, 63 **Ch 5** Drawing the Body of the Guitar, 91 **Ch 5** Drawing the Bridge and Strings of the Guitar, 96	**4.1** Creating the Streets **5.2** Using the Pen Tool to Draw the Shape of the Guitar **5.4** Adding the Bridge Details and Strings **6.4** Saving to Web-Based Formats Using the Save For Web Command
4.2 Add and manipulate text using appropriate typographic settings.	**Ch 5** Placing Text and Linking Text Areas, 111 **Ch 6** Adding Text and Photos, 122	**3.3** Adding Text for the Logotype of the Business Card **5.7** Distorting Objects Using the Envelope Distort Feature **6.3** Adding Text and Images to the Mobile Mockup
4.2a Use a variety of tools to add typography to a design.	**Ch 2** Adding Text to the Postcard, 39 **Ch 3** Adding Text for the Logotype, 52	**2.7** Using the Type Tool to Add Text Elements to the Postcard **3.3** Adding Text for the Logotype of the Business Card **4.5** Adding names to each street on the map
4.2b Use appropriate character settings in a design	**Ch 3** Adding Text for the Logotype, 52	**3.3** Adding Text for the Logotype of the Business Card **5.9** Placing Text from an External File
4.2c Use appropriate paragraph settings in a design.	**Ch 3** Adding Text for the Logotype, 52 **Ch 3** Adding Paragraph Text to the Front of the Business Card, 58	**3.3** Adding Text for the Logotype of the Business Card **3.7** Adding Paragraph Text to the Front of the Business Card
4.2d Convert text to graphics.	**Ch 3** Customizing the Logotype, 56	**3.5** Converting the Logotype Text to Paths **5.6** Running Image Trace on an Image
4.2e Manage text flow across multiple text areas.	**Ch 5** Placing Text and Linking Text Areas, 111	**5.9** Placing Text from an External File
4.3 Make, manage, and manipulate selections.	**Ch 2** Drawing the Basic Lemon Artwork, 42	

continues on next page

continued from previous page

DOMAIN OBJECTIVES	CHAPTER	VIDEO
4.3a Make selections using a variety of tools.	**Ch 4** Selecting Objects and Working with Groups, 67 **Ch 4** Working with Layers, 73	**4.2** Selecting Based on Appearance and Working with Groups **4.4** Organizing the Content on the Back of the Card Using Layers
4.3b Modify and refine selections using various methods.	**Ch 2** Drawing the Basic Lemon Artwork, 42 **Ch 4** Selecting Objects and Working with Groups, 67	**2.8** Drawing a Lemon Using Basic Shape Tools in Adobe Illustrator CC **4.2** Selecting Based on Appearance and Working with Groups
4.3c Group or ungroup selections.	**Ch 3** Customizing the Logotype, 56 **Ch 4** Selecting Objects and Working with Groups, 67 **Ch 5** Using Image Trace to Create Distressed Text, 103	**3.5** Converting the Logotype Text to Paths **4.2** Selecting Based on Appearance and Working with Groups
4.4 Transform digital graphics and media.	**Ch 6** Creating the Icons for the Mobile Mockup, 117	**6.2** Creating the Icons for the Mobile Mockup
4.4a Modify artboards.	**Ch 3** Modifying an Artboard, 47	**3.1** Modifying Artboards
4.4b Rotate, flip, and transform individual layers, objects, selections, groups, or graphical elements.	**Ch 3** Finishing Up the Business Card Front, 59 **Ch 4** Creating and Applying a Pattern Swatch, 79 **Ch 5** Adding the Frets and Fret Markers to the Neck of the Guitar, 94 **Ch 5** Using Envelope Distort to Distort Text to a Specific Shape, 107	**3.8** Finishing Up the Front of the Card **4.6** Creating a Pattern Swatch for the Landmarks **5.3** Drawing the Frets and Fret Markers on the Guitar **5.7** Distorting Objects Using the Envelope Distort Feature
4.5 Use basic reconstructing and editing techniques to manipulate digital graphics and media.	**Ch 5** Drawing the Body of the Guitar, 91	**5.2** Using the Pen Tool to Draw the Shape of the Guitar
4.5a Apply basic auto-correction methods and tools.	**Ch 2** Drawing a Shape Using the Shaper Tool, 35 **Ch 4** Drawing the Streets of the Map, 63 **Ch 4** Adding a Gradient Effect and Details to the Landmarks, 81	**2.4** Creating Shapes for the Background of the Postcard Project **4.1** Creating the Streets **4.7** Adding a Gradient Effect to the Landmarks

DOMAIN OBJECTIVES	CHAPTER	VIDEO
4.5b Use various tools to repair and reconstruct images.	**Ch 3** Creating a Half-Pipe for the Background of the Card, 50 **Ch 5** Using Envelope Distort to Distort Text to a Specific Shape, 107 **Ch 6** Creating the Icons for the Mobile Mockup, 117	**3.2** Creating a Half-Pipe for the Business Card **3.6** Using Live Paint to Enhance the Logotype **4.1** Creating the Streets **6.2** Creating the Icons for the Mobile Mockup
4.5c Evaluate or adjust appearance of objects, selections, or layers using various tools.	**Ch 2** Creating Shapes for the Postcard Background, 34 **Ch 4** Using the Appearance Panel, 70 **Ch 4** Adding a Gradient Effect and Details to the Landmarks, 81	**2.4** Creating Shapes for the Background of the Postcard Project **4.3** Using the Appearance Panel to Add an Appearance to the Streets **4.7** Adding a Gradient Effect to the Landmarks
4.5d Use Image Trace to create a vector from a bitmap graphic.	**Ch 5** Using Image Trace to Create Distressed Text, 103	**5.6** Running Image Trace on an Image
4.6 Modify design elements using effects and graphic styles.	**Ch 4** Creating a Graphic Style, 71	**4.3** Using the Appearance Panel to Add an Appearance to the Streets
4.6a Use Effects to modify images.	**Ch 5** Adding Effects to the Music Poster, 109	**5.8** Adding Effects to the Music Poster
4.6b Create, edit, and save Graphic Styles.	**Ch 4** Working with Layers, 73	**4.3** Using the Appearance Panel to Add an Appearance to the Streets **4.4** Organizing the Content on the Back of the Card Using Layers
4.6c Expand Appearance of objects.	**Ch 4** Using the Appearance Panel, 70 **Ch 6** Creating the Icons for the Mobile Mockup, 117	**6.2** Creating the Icons for the Mobile Mockup
DOMAIN 5.0 Publishing Digital Media		
5.1 Prepare images for export to web, print, and video.	**Ch 1** Saving and Exporting Files, 21	**1.4** Saving and Exporting Documents
5.2 Export or save digital images to various file formats.	**Ch 1** Saving and Exporting Files, 21 **Ch 6** Creating Web Graphics Using Save For Web, 124 **Ch 6** Using Export for Screens to Generate Web and Mobile Assets, 127	**1.4** Saving and Exporting Documents

continues on next page

continued from previous page

DOMAIN OBJECTIVES	CHAPTER	VIDEO
5.2a Save in the native file format for Illustrator (.ai).	**Ch 1** Saving and Exporting Files, 21	**1.4** Saving and Exporting Documents
5.2b Save in appropriate image formats for print or screen.	**Ch 6** Creating a Document for a Mobile Device, 115	**6.1** Creating an Illustrator File at the Size of a Mobile Screen **6.4** Saving to Web-Based Formats Using the Save For Web Command
5.2c Export project elements.	**Ch 6** Using Export for Screens to Generate Web and Mobile Assets, 127	**6.5** Using Export for Screens to Create Assets for Web and Mobile Use
5.2d Package an Illustrator project	**Ch 5** Packaging the Project, 112	**5.10** Packaging the Elements of the Project for Distribution

Glossary

additive color Color created by combining light. Color components are red, green, and blue. When added together at 100%, the three components create white.

Adobe Bridge An Adobe application that enables you to view thumbnails of your files and helps you sort and organize those files. It gives you centralized access to all your Illustrator files and to other media assets you may need for your projects. In Illustrator, the Go To Bridge button is located on the Application bar.

alignment Indicates how the lines are aligned on the right and left edges, such as left, centered, and right.

all caps Uses only uppercase letterforms for each letter.

analogous (colors) Colors that are side by side on the color wheel. They create gentle and relaxing color schemes.

anchor point A point connecting two segments on a path. An anchor point can be either a corner point or a curved point. See also *corner point* and *smooth anchor point*.

appearance The attributes that are applied to an object and that are listed on the Appearance panel.

Application bar The bar at the top of the Application frame. The bar contains the Go To Bridge button, the Arrange Documents menu, the Workspace switcher menu, and the Search for Help field. In Windows, the main Illustrator menus also appear on this bar.

Application frame The frame that surrounds the Illustrator interface and contains the Application bar, document windows, and panels, as well as select zoom and artboard navigation options.

area type A type object (consisting of many lines of text) where type wraps to fit within a vector shape.

Arrange Documents menu Located on the Application bar, this menu allows you to view multiple document windows in a variety of horizontal or vertical arrangements within the Application frame.

artboard The working area in a document. Artwork placed on an artboard will appear in the final output (printed or onscreen). The dimensions of the artboard define the size of the output. An Illustrator file can contain up to 100 artboards.

asymmetrical Achieves balance using elements with different weights or values on each side (or the top and bottom) of an image.

attributes The settings such as fill, stroke, effects, and opacity that are applied to an object. The attributes of an object make up the object's appearance.

attribution Written acknowledgment provided with the name of the original copyright holder of the work. Creative Commons and other licenses feature different kinds of attribution requirements.

balance Evenly distributed, but not necessarily centered or mirrored.

baseline An imaginary line used to organize text along a horizontal plane.

bitmap An image created by a grid of pixels with each pixel assigned a color and, in some file formats (PNG and GIF), a transparency value.

blackletter fonts Ornate and antique-looking typefaces; also known as Old English or Gothic. Convey a feeling of rich and sophisticated gravitas.

bleed The part of the image extending past the cut edge to ensure an edge-to-edge print.

blending mode Determines how a layer or object blends with the layers beneath it, such as Darken, Soft Light, or Difference.

canvas The working area in Illustrator that surrounds the artboards. The canvas can be used as a temporary pasteboard to hold graphics, text, or other design elements.

cast shadow The shadow cast by a form. Shadows fade with distance from the form.

chaotic A description of lines or shapes that appear disorganized and messy. Convey a sense of urgency, fear, or explosive energy.

clipping mask A special group of objects in which the topmost object crops (masks) the objects that are below it. Portions of the lower objects that extend beyond the path of the topmost object are hidden and don't print. The topmost object in a clipping mask is referred to as a clipping path.

color The perceived hue, lightness, and saturation of an object or light.

color harmonies Color rules that are named for their relative locations on the color wheel.

color mode For each particular document, this determines how the components of a color are combined, based on the number of color channels in the document's color model, such as RGB or CYMK.

complementary (colors) Colors that are opposite each other on the color wheel. They are high in contrast and vibrant.

compound path An object contained within one or more smaller, transparent paths that creates a hole in the larger object. The hole can be removed by releasing the compound object and separating the paths into individual objects.

compound shape An object created via the Shape Modes options on the Pathfinder panel. The individual objects that are combined into a compound shape are preserved and can be edited or released at any time.

contrast Quality that creates visual interest in a composition using variety. It draws the eye to the focal point.

Control panel A horizontal panel at the top of the Illustrator interface that contains controls, links (to temporary panels), and settings. Options on the panel change depending on the type of object currently selected.

convert a point Change an anchor point from corner to curved, or vice versa. You can convert points via the Anchor Point tool or via options on the Control panel.

corner point An anchor point whose direction handles do not form a symmetrical, straight line. Corner points can connect two straight line segments, a straight and a curved segment, or two curved segments on a path.

Creative Cloud Libraries A feature provided in Illustrator that enables you to copy artwork as an asset into a Libraries panel and then place that asset into any other Adobe application that also contains a Libraries panel. Library assets are stored in your Creative Cloud Assets page.

Creative Commons Ways that artists can release their works for limited use and still choose the way the works are used and shared: Public Domain, Attribution, ShareAlike, NoDerivs, and NonCommercial.

curved (line) Expresses fluidity, beauty, and grace.

decorative fonts Also known as ornamental, novelty, or display fonts. They don't fall into any of the other categories of fonts. Convey a specific feeling.

deliverables A predetermined list of items that will be delivered to the customer.

desaturate Remove the amount of color in an image.

design elements The building blocks of art defined by artists to provide a framework for creating art.

diagonal (lines) Lines traveling on neither a vertical nor a horizontal path. Express growth or decline and imply movement or change.

dingbat fonts Also known as wingdings. They are a collection of objects and shapes instead of letters.

direction A common way to describe lines, such as vertical, horizontal, or diagonal.

direction handle A visual feature that displays on a selected curved anchor point that controls the shape of a curved segment.

dock The vertically stacked arrangements of panels on the right side of the Application frame. You can customize the arrangement of panels in the dock and create additional docks.

document color mode Determines the color model that Illustrator uses to create the image, such as RGB or CYMK.

document window A tabbed window within the Application frame that contains the artboards and canvas scratch area.

drawing modes Illustrator provides three specific drawing modes: Draw Normal (the default), Draw Behind, and Draw Inside. Draw Behind places newly drawn objects behind selected objects. Draw Inside places newly drawn objects within a selected object.

edge The boundary between two faces in a *Live Paint* group.

elements of art The building blocks of creative works. They are the "nouns" of design, such as space, line, shape, form, texture, value, color, and type.

embedding Placing a bitmap image as a non-vector object in an Illustrator document. The image data is stored in the document. See also *linking*.

emphasis Describes the focal point to which the eye is naturally and initially drawn in a design.

face In Illustrator, the area formed by intersecting lines in a *Live Paint* group.

fair use A set of rules that specify how and when copyrighted material can be used and that make sure copyright protection doesn't come at the cost of creativity and freedom.

feedback loop A system set up to continually encourage and require input and approval on a project's direction.

fill Solid color, pattern, or gradient that is applied to the interior of a vector object. The current fill color displays in the Fill square on several panels in Illustrator.

flow In a design, the energy conveyed by lines and shapes.

focal point What the design is all about. The call to action or the primary message you are trying to get across.

fonts The whole collection of a typeface in each of its sizes and styles.

form Describes three-dimensional objects, such as spheres, cubes, and pyramids.

geometric (lines) Tend to be straight and have sharp angles. Look manmade and intentional. Communicate strength, power, and precision.

geometric shapes Predictable and consistent shapes, such as circles, squares, triangles, and stars. They are rarely found in nature and convey mechanical and manufactured impressions.

GIF Graphics Interchange Format: A lossless bitmap image format limited to 256 colors; supports animation.

glyph Each character of a font, whether it is a letter, number, symbol, or swash.

gradient fill A gradual blend between two or more solid colors. Gradients are created and edited via the Gradient panel in Illustrator.

graphic style A set of Appearance panel properties saved as a preset.

group A collection of objects on an artboard that can be selected as an entire unit for editing and organizing elements in a design. On the Layers panel, a <Group> listing will display, and the collection of objects will display as individual listings nested within the group.

hand-drawn (line or shape) Appears as though created using traditional techniques, such as paints, charcoal, or chalk.

handwritten font A typeface that simulates handwriting.

highlight The area of a form that is directly facing the light and that appears lightest.

horizontal Moving from left to right; for example, the horizontal line in an "H." Expresses calmness and balance.

horizontal scale Describes the function of stretching letters and distorting the typeface geometry.

hue The actual color of an element (such as red, blue, or green).

hyphenation Splitting words with hyphens when wrapping to the next line.

ideographs (ideograms) Images that represent an idea, such as a heart representing love.

implied line Doesn't really exist but is implied by a shape, such as a dotted or dashed line, people waiting in line, or the margin of a block of text.

indent Settings that determine how far an entire paragraph is set back from the rest of the text on each side or in just its first line.

isolation mode A special viewing and editing mode that is activated by double-clicking an object or a group. All other objects are temporarily dimmed, thereby limiting editing to only the selected objects.

iterations New versions of a design that successively become closer to the desired result.

iterative work Work that is shared as it is completed, allowing the customer to chime in with comments while it is still easy to make a change.

join To unite two endpoints into one point on a path. Points can be joined via the Join tool.

JPG or JPEG Joint Photographic Experts Group A lossy bitmap image format, suitable for complex or continuous tone images like photographs.

justified Aligning text to a straight edge on both the right and left edges of a paragraph.

kerning The space between specific letter pairs.

layers A way to organize objects and put some objects in front of, or behind, others. When objects are on separate layers, you can manipulate one item without affecting another, even if the two are in the same area of the image.

leading The amount of space between the baselines of two lines of text, like double-spaced text.

licensing A way to legally use copyrighted material for a certain time and in a certain way, usually associated with paying a fee established by the copyright holder.

ligatures Special characters used to represent letter combinations, such as "fi."

light source The perceived location of the lighting in relation to the form.

lightness A color setting affecting tone, from darker to lighter.

line A mark with a beginning and an end point.

linking Placing a bitmap image as a screen version of an image in an Illustrator document. A link is established between the placed image and the original source image. Image data is not stored in the document. See also *embedding*.

Live Corners A feature that allows you to reshape any corner point on a path. When the path is selected with the Direct Selection tool, Live Corner widgets appear at each corner point. Drag the widget to reshape the corner point interactively.

Live Paint A feature that lets you apply different colors to different parts of an object. After an object is converted to a Live Paint group, it is composed of *faces* and *edges*.

Live Shapes A feature for rectangle or rounded rectangle objects only that displays corner widgets for controlling the corner radius on a selected object. See also *shape properties*.

metadata Information that is included in a document but that is hidden, such as copyright, lens information, location via GPS, camera settings, and more.

model release The permission that is required when a person's face is identifiable in a photo and the image will be used to promote something—whether it's a product or an idea.

monochromatic Different shades and tints of the same color. Communicates a relaxed and peaceful feeling.

monospaced fonts Fixed-width or nonproportional fonts that use the same amount of horizontal space for each letter.

movement Visual movement within an image, such as the natural tracking of the eye across an image as the eye moves from focal point to focal point.

negative space Blank areas in a design. Also known as white space.

NoDerivs Creative Commons licensing. Requires that you not change material when you incorporate it into your own work. It can be used freely, but you must pass it along without change.

NonCommercial Creative Commons licensing. Means you can use work in your own creative work as long as you don't charge for it.

opacity The inverse of transparency, or the degree to which an object obscures objects beneath it in the layer stack.

object Any created vector shape or placed image in an Illustrator document. An individual object can be selected for editing and is listed on the Layers panel as a <Path>.

object shadow The area of the form that is facing away from the light source and appears darkest.

organic Describes lines, shapes, or forms that are irregular and imperfect, as those found in nature.

organic shapes Are random or generated by something natural. They are usually asymmetric and convey natural, homemade, or relaxed feelings.

panel This highly customizable area containing common tools in the interface that can be easily moved, rearranged, or resized.

panel group A tabbed grouping of multiple panels, usually located in a dock.

paragraph settings Affect an entire paragraph rather than selected words. These settings include alignment, space before or after, hyphenation, and so on.

paragraph spacing Similar to leading but applies to the spacing above or below the entire paragraph (and not to the lines within the paragraph).

paragraph type A type object (consisting of many lines of text) where the type wraps to fit within a text rectangle.

path The edge of a vector shape or line. A path technically has no dimension, so a stroke must be added to make it visible.

path type A type object containing type that follows the edge of an object's path.

pattern A repetitive sequence of different colors or shape objects. You can use the Pattern Options panel to create custom patterns that can be applied as a fill or stroke on a path.

pictograph (pictogram) Graphic symbol that represents something in the real world. Computer icons are pictographs that suggest the function they represent, such as a trash can icon for deleting a file.

pixel A single dot that makes up a raster image. Pixel is short for "picture element."

Place command The main method for bringing external files into an Illustrator document.

PNG or Portable Network Graphics A lossless bitmap image format useful for both complex photographic elements and simpler images. PNG images may use 8-bit color (PNG-8) or 24-bit color (PNG-24) and may include a full alpha channel, allowing for nuanced transparency.

point type A type object (consisting of just one character or several words of text) that stands by itself and is not associated with any drawn path or object. Point type can be positioned anywhere on an artboard.

points Used to measure type size, approximately 1/72 of an inch.

ppi Stands for "pixels per inch." Higher ppi affords more detail. While vector objects are resolution independent, raster effects and rasterized objects and images need to have a ppi value defined for output.

Preferences dialog box A dialog box that contains various options and settings that are applied to all Illustrator documents you create. The dialog box organizes the options and settings into specific categories and displays each category in a custom panel. Preference settings can be changed at any time.

primary colors Colors that cannot be created by combining other colors, and that can be combined to create every other color in the visible spectrum. Additive color systems such as a computer use the primary colors of red, blue, and green (not red, blue, and yellow as in painting).

principles of design The essential rules governing art. In short, a design should have a focal point, and the rest of the elements of the design should support, and draw attention to, that focal point.

process colors Colors that are defined as a combination of the four CMYK (Cyan, Magenta, Yellow, and Black) ink colors. Process colors are used when printing artwork to devices that create color using these four inks.

project creep Unplanned changes that increase the amount of work, or scope, that a project requires. When the project loses focus and spins out of control, it eats up more and more time and effort.

project deadlines Dictates when work needs to be completed.

project scope Outlines the amount and type of work to be completed.

proportion (scale) Describes the relative size, number, and scale of elements in a design.

proportionally An option that can be set when scaling an object to preserve the current width-to-height ratio of an object.

Public Domain Creative Commons licensing. When copyright is expired or released and no longer applies to the content or when artist release their work. It can be used without worrying about infringement.

radial Circular type of balance among elements distributed around the center of a design.

raster Originally described an image created by scan lines on CRT monitors, but today it is basically synonymous with bitmap. Certain effects in Illustrator are referred to as "raster" because they are composed of pixels and not vector shapes.

rasterize To convert a vector object into a raster/bitmap image.

reflected highlight Area of a form that is lit by reflections from the ground or other objects in a scene.

render To convert a nonraster image or effect into a raster image.

repetition Repeating an element in a design.

representative shape A shape used to convey information pictorially. Such shapes are helpful in communicating with multicultural and multilingual audiences.

resolution A measurement of the number of pixels in a given space—either on a per-inch basis (ppi) or pixel dimensions (such as 1920x1080).

rhythm Creative and expressive, rather than a consistent pattern or repetition in a design.

rule of thirds A technique for laying out the space of your page to provide a focal point. Two vertical and two horizontal lines evenly divide the space into nine equal boxes, as in a tic-tac-toe board.

sans serif fonts Text without serifs. Often used for headlines and titles for their strong, stable, modern feel.

saturation The level of pure color versus white or gray in a color. Less white or gray means a more vivid, or saturated, color.

script fonts Mimic calligraphy. They convey a feeling of beauty, grace, or feminine dignity.

secondary colors Created when you combine primary colors.

serif fonts Fonts with serifs, the little "feet" on character ends, created by type-writers. They convey tradition, intelligence, and class.

shape Area enclosed or defined by an outline, such as geometric shapes or hand-drawn shapes. In Illustrator, shapes are also referred to as objects when talking about the actual elements in the artwork.

shape properties The middle portion of the Transform panel that displays shape and corner settings for a selected object drawn with the Rectangle or Rounded Rectangle tool. See also *Live Shapes*.

ShareAlike Creative Commons licensing. Allows you to use an item (design) in any way you want as long as your creation is shared under the same license as the original work.

sketches Representative drawings of how to lay out a document or web page. These are sometimes one of the deliverables of a project.

slab serif fonts Squared-off versions of a typical serif font. Also known as Egyptian, block serif, or square serif. Convey a machine-built feel.

slice An area of an Illustrator file defined as an element in a web design.

small caps Uses only uppercase letterforms for each letter and appears in a smaller size.

smooth anchor point An anchor point that connects two curved segments that connect in a continuous curve. Direction handles for a smooth point always move in tandem to preserve the smoothness of the curve. See *anchor point*.

Smooth curve Two segments that create a continuous curve on either side of a smooth anchor point.

space The canvas, or working area. Its dimensions are determined by the resolution of the page you are creating.

specifications Detailed written goals and limits for a project. These are sometimes one of the deliverables of a project.

stock photos Images for which the author retains copyright but for which a license for use is available.

stroke Solid color, pattern, or gradient applied to the edge of a vector object. To make the stroke visible, a weight (width) and color need to be applied to the object. The current stroke color displays in the Stroke square on several panels in Illustrator.

stroke weight The thickness (width) applied to a stroke on the edge of a path.

style (line) An effect applied to a line, such as varying width, hand-drawn, and implied.

subtractive color The familiar model of mixing red, yellow, and blue ink or paint to make colors. Cyan, magenta, yellow, and black inks (CMYK) are used in standard printing. We see the colors because the opaque pigments or inks block certain wavelengths of light and let others through.

SVG or Scalable Vector Graphics A vector graphic format supported by modern web browsers.

swashes Special characters with flowing and elegant endings for the ascenders and descenders.

swatch A saved and named color, tint, gradient, or pattern. Swatches can be exported and shared using swatch libraries.

symbol A predefined, reusable design element accessed via the Symbols panel.

symmetrical Occurs when you can divide an image along its middle, and the left side of the image is a mirror image of the right (or the top reflects the bottom). Conveys an intentional, formal, and mechanical feeling.

template layer A locked nonprinting layer that hold images for tracing.

tertiary colors Created by mixing primary and secondary colors.

texture Describes the actual tactile texture in real objects or the appearance of texture in a two-dimensional image.

Tools panel Contains all the tools that you can use in Illustrator. Most icons on the toolbar provide access to a group of hidden tools when you click and hold on the tool's icon.

trace Convert shapes in a bitmap image into vector paths. In Illustrator, this can be done manually via the Pen tool or automatically via the Image Trace feature.

tracking The overall space between all the letters in a block of text. It allows you to compress or expand the space between the letters as a whole rather than just between specific pairs, as you do with kerning.

type size A font's height from the highest ascender to the lowest descender.

typeface Specific letterform set, such as Helvetica, Arial, Garamond, and so on. It is the "look" of letters.

unity Also known as harmony and sharing similar traits. Low contrast. Things that go together should look like they belong together. The opposite of variety.

value Lightness or darkness of an object. Together with color, represents the visible spectrum, such as a gradient.

variable width profile Preset and user-defined settings displayed on the Profile menu and in the Stroke panel applied to an object's stroke.

variable width stroke A stroke that does not have a uniform width. In Illustrator, use the Variable Width Profile menu (on the Control panel) or the Width tool to create a variable width stroke.

variety High contrast. The opposite of unity.

varying-width (line) Expresses flow and grace.

vector object An element composed of points connected by straight and curved segments defined by mathematical instructions. Vector object are resolution independent. This means they can be scaled with no loss of edge quality.

vertical scale Describes the function of stretching letters and distorting the typeface geometry.

weight (stroke) The thickness, or width, of a line.

wireframe A schematic sketch of a project, commonly used for interactive projects.

Workspace switcher menu The menu, located on the Application bar, that enables you to choose predefine workspaces and save user-defined, customized workspaces.

workspaces Specific arrangements of the panels within the interface for easy access to features you use often. Illustrator provides predefined workspaces, or you can create a custom workspace that suits your workflow needs.

Index

Command key. *See* keyboard
    shortcuts
communication, importance of,
    187–188
complementary colors, 155
compound path, 106, 108.
    See also paths
contrast, principle of,
    135–136, 167
Control panel, 35
copyrights, 180–185
corner radius, changing for shapes,
    36–37, 98
counter, typography, 161
Creative Cloud Libraries,
    showing items in, 7. *See also*
    Libraries panel
Creative Commons licensing,
    184–185
creativity
    graph of, 132
    prepping mind, 133
    and thoughts, 190
Ctrl key. *See* keyboard shortcuts
curved lines, 66–67, 144. *See also*
    lines
customers. *See* clients

D

deadlines, 191
decorative fonts, 160
deleting
    portion of ellipse, 64
    workspaces, 21
deliverables, 192
demographic, targeting for clients,
    178
desaturation, 123
descender, typography, 161
deselecting tools, 13
design hierarchy, 133–137
design principles. *See also*
    principles of design
    balance, 169–170
    contrast, 167
    emphasis, 166–167
    focal point, 166–167
    movement and rhythm, 172
    overview, 165–166
    pattern swatch, 171
    proportion, 171
    repetition, 171
    scale, 171
    unity, 167–168
    variety, 168–169

diagonal lines, 143
dingbat fonts, 161
Direct Selection tool, 42, 68, 93.
    See also Selection tool
direction handles, adjusting, 92
direction of lines, 143
display fonts, 160
distorting text, 107–108.
    See also text
distressed text, creating, 106–107
docking panels, 9, 17–19
document color mode, 10
Document Info section, 8, 10
document tabs, 8
document window, 9
documents
    changing properties, 13–14
    creating, 10–11
    creating for postcard, 27–30
    customizing settings, 11–14
    mobile devices, 115–116
    navigating, 37–38
    presets, 11
    resizing, 14
    saving, 30
    searching, 7
    settings, 29
drawing
    body of guitar, 91–93
    curved streets, 66–67
    lemon artwork, 42–43
    lines, 44
    neck of guitar, 93
    paths, 96
    with Pen tool, 92
    rectangles, 34–35, 51, 107
    shapes, 35
    skateboard for business card,
        59–61
    streets of map, 63–67
    string pegs and bridge, 97–98
    strings for guitar, 99
    triangle, 45
drop shadow, adding to Text
    Background layer, 110

E

edges, Live Paint group, 57
education, considering in
    demographics, 178
effects, adding to music poster,
    109–110
Egyptian fonts, 160

elements of art
    colors, 152–157
    explained, 133
    forms, 147–149
    lines, 142–145
    overview, 138
    patterns and textures, 149–150
    shapes, 145–147
    space, 139–141
    type, 157–164
    values, 151–152
elevator pitches, 177
ellipse
    deleting portion, 64
    scaling pattern in, 81
Ellipse tool, 42–43, 64, 80
embedding images, 90
emphasis, principle of, 166–167
Envelope Distort, 107–108
.eps file format, 22
Eraser tool, 64, 74
Essentials Classic workspace, 15
evaluating and testing
    projects, 194
Export For Screens, 127–128
exporting
    assets, 128
    and saving files, 21–24
    web image assets, 125–126
Eyedropper tool, 82–83

F

face, Live Paint group, 57
failure, taking in stride, 133
fair use policy, 182–183
favorites, dragging to Asset Export
    panel, 128
feedback loop, 194
feeling
    creating, 140
    design hierarchy, 137
    and texture, 150
files
    opening, 6–7
    saving and exporting, 21–24
fill
    adding to shapes, 81–83
    indicator, 34
    options, 9
Film & Video option for
    documents, 11, 29
finial, typography, 161
fixed-width fonts, 160
floating panels, 16–17

flow
of lines, 144
of shapes, 146
focal point, principle of, 135, 166–167
Font Family menu, 41
fonts
activating, 7
explained, 158
ligatures and swashes, 163
Typekit, 39
form, element of, 147–149
formal fonts, 160
formatting text, 40–42
frets and fret markers, adding to guitar, 94–96

G

geometric lines, 144
GIF (Graphics Interchange Format), 125
glyphs, 160
Golden Rule for client projects, 179
Gothic fonts, 160
gradient effect, adding, 81–83
graphic styles
applying, 76–77
creating, 71–72
updating, 72–73
grids, showing, 14
Group Selection tool, 68
grouping objects, 67–68
groups
editing contents, 69
selecting, 42
working with, 68–69
guides, using, 14, 32–34
guitar
applying color, 92–93
bridge and strings, 96–99
drawing body, 91–93
drawing neck, 93
drawing strings, 99
frets and fret markers, 94–96

H

half-pipe
creating, 50–51
positioning skateboard, 60–61
Hand tool, 38
hand-drawn lines, 144
handwritten fonts, 160
Harmony Rules menu, 55
Help, searching, 7
highlight, 3D lighting, 148

hobbies, considering in demographics, 178
horizontal lines, 143
horizontal scale, 163
hue, 153
hyphenation, 164

I

icons, creating for mobile mockup, 117–121
ideal customer, identifying, 178–179
ideas, iterations, 190
ideographs/ideograms, 146
Illustrator. *See* Adobe Illustrator CC
Illustrator EPS file format, 22
Illustrator Options dialog box, 23
Illustrator Template file format, 22
Image Trace, running, 104–105
images. *See also* photos
linking and embedding, 90
placing, 89–91
placing and sizing, 104
sizing on artboard, 90
implied lines, 144–145
inches, changing units to, 30
income, considering in demographics, 178
indent settings, 164
interface, creating for mobile devices, 116
isolation mode, 69, 107
italics, 167
iterations of ideas, 190

J

Join tool, 65–66
JPEG (Joint Photographic Experts Group) format, 124–125
justified text, 164

K

kaleidoscopic image, 170
kerning and tracking, 52–54, 161–162
keyboard shortcuts
graphic styles, 73
guides, 32
kerning, 53
Shape Builder tool, 51
Spotlight, 38
tracking, 53
Zoom tool, 38
Knife tool, 64

L

Landmarks layer, 75
launching, Adobe Illustrator CC, 4–5
layers. *See also* template layer
creating, 91
targeting, 110
working with, 73–77
Layers panel, nested groups, 68
leading, typography, 42, 161–162
Learn and Work modes, toggling, 7
legacy, adding to Save For Web, 125
lemon
drawing artwork, 42–43
embellishing, 44–45
Libraries panel, 19. *See also* Creative Cloud Libraries
licensing, 184–185
ligature, typography, 161, 163
light source, 3D lighting, 148
lightness, 153
Line tool, 64, 94
lines. *See also* curved lines
copying, 94
drawing, 44
element of, 142–145
linking images, 90
Links folder, 112
Live Corners, 36
Live Paint Bucket tool, 56–57
Live Shapes, 36
logotype
adding text, 52–54
interleaving shapes, 56–57
loop, typography, 161
Lorem ipsum, 40

M

manager, thinking like, 186–195
Maps symbol library, 85
menu bar, 8
message and voice, unifying, 176–178
metadata, adding to digital files, 182
mobile assets, generating, 127–128
mobile devices
assets, 127–128
divisions of main screen, 122–123
document, 115–116
icons, 117–120
interface, 116
Reference point icon, 122